SCHOLASTIC

Nonfiction Literacy-Building Booklets & Activities

Lucia Kemp Henry & Suzanne Moore

NEW YORK • TORONTO • LONDON • AUCKLAND • SYDNEY
MEXICO CITY • NEW DELHI • HONG KONG • BUENOS AIRES

Teaching *Resources*

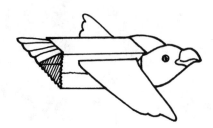

Cover design by Maria Lilja
Interior design by Sydney Wright
Cover and interior illustrations by Lucia Kemp Henry

ISBN-13: 978-0-439-56721-3
ISBN-10: 0-439-56721-1

2 3 4 5 6 7 8 9 10   40   15 14 13 12 11 10 09

Contents

(continued)

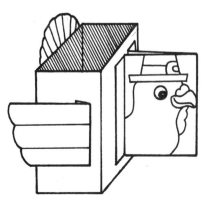

Contents

Introduction

Welcome to *Nonfiction Literacy-Building Booklets & Activities*—a delightful collection of fun activities, easy-to-make booklets, and unique projects designed to help children build vocabulary and literacy skills as they explore a variety of social studies topics.

The interactive activities in *Nonfiction Literacy-Building Booklets & Activities* offer fresh, engaging opportunities to strengthen early literacy skills by exposing children to key concepts of print. By making and "reading" these booklets and projects, children begin to understand that:

- print carries meaning
- words are read top to bottom and left to right
- letters create particular sounds
- reading should be careful and even-paced

The booklets and projects facilitate vocabulary development by exploring important social studies concepts and favorite themes throughout the year. The activities also provide children with repeated opportunities to listen, speak, and follow directions, thereby improving their oral language skills. You can use the activities to introduce nonfiction topics, teach new concepts, and reinforce previously learned information, as well as boost vocabulary, explore concepts of print, build background knowledge, and much more!

Nonfiction Literacy-Building Booklets & Activities is packed with reproducible pattern pages that make preparation of booklets and projects a breeze. For most activities, simply copy the pattern pages for each child, collect the art materials listed, and you're ready to go! As children color, cut, glue, and write to make the booklets and other projects, they'll be intrigued by the engaging formats—lift-the-flap activities, shape books, flip books, accordion books—and will also develop their fine motor skills.

But completing the activities is only half the fun! After constructing their booklets and projects, invite children to use them to share their content knowledge with classmates, family members, and friends. Also, children might help create classroom displays with some of their projects. With these hands-on activities, you'll provide children with numerous opportunities to learn important concepts and develop critical skills needed for future learning.

About This Book

What's Inside?

Each project in *Nonfiction Literacy-Building Booklets & Activities* focuses on a specific topic or theme. To help you find the perfect activity, each topic is conveniently categorized under one of these sections: Neighborhood & Community, Our Country, and Celebrations Around the World. In addition, topics are organized under subcategories for each section. For instance, We All Live Together, Around the Neighborhood, and Around and About are found in the Neighborhood & Community section. The projects are independent of each other, so they can be used in any order to fit your instructional needs. For every topic, you'll find a teaching page that includes the following:

Facts to Share

You can share these important and interesting facts with children as you introduce and discuss the topic. But don't limit yourself to only the information provided in this section. You might research books, the Internet, and other resources to build your own background knowledge—especially in less familiar topics—and to gather additional information, facts, pictures, and so on to share with children.

Introducing the Activity

Use the activity in this section to introduce the topic to children—and set the stage for making the related booklet or project. The activity helps you tap into children's prior knowledge, build background knowledge, and expand vocabulary.

Materials

Check this section to find what materials each child will need to complete the booklet or project. The reproducible pattern pages listed for most activities make your preparation time minimal. Many projects require basic art supplies including crayons, scissors, glue sticks, and construction paper. Some use additional craft items such as paint, wiggle eyes, yarn, paper lunch bags, and paper plates. Most likely these materials are already in your supply cabinet. To make binding the booklets fast and simple, have a few staplers on hand.

What to Do

This section includes easy, step-by-step directions for making and assembling the booklets and projects. You might want to make each project in advance to become familiar with the steps, as well as to have a sample to show children.

Extension Activity

The activities in this section compliment and enrich student learning about the topic or theme. They provide engaging opportunities to reinforce important concepts, strengthen literacy skills, and broaden learning.

Book Break

Suggestions for topic-related nonfiction books are provided along with a brief summary of the books. Read or review the books ahead of time to become familiar with their content and illustrations. As you share facts and other information from the books, you might paraphrase or summarize some parts to help children better understand the content.

Also, you might explore with children what a nonfiction author does and how information is communicated in a nonfiction book. For instance, the author does a lot of research and writes about something that is real or historical. And a nonfiction book might include text features such as a table of contents, glossary, index, photographs, captions, maps, tables and charts, diagrams, and sidebars.

Song or Poem

Many of the activities include a song, rhyme, or poem designed to reinforce specific concepts, skills, or knowledge-building information in a fun and engaging way. The songs are set to the tune of familiar childhood songs and the poems follow simple rhyme patterns. Before using each song or rhyme, you might practice singing or reciting it to become familiar with the tune or rhythm.

Building Literacy Skills With the Songs and Poems

Use these ideas to further enhance and enrich children's literacy skills:

- Copy the song or poem onto chart paper. Invite children to identify specific letters, beginning sounds, or words on the chart. You might also leave out words as you sing or recite the verses and have children fill in the missing words.

- Write each line of a song or poem onto a separate sentence strip. Challenge children to sequence the sentence strips and then sing or recite the lines.

- After singing a song or reciting a poem, invite children to make up additional lines or verses.

- Have children replace key words in the lines of a song or poem to give it new meaning. Or invite them to alter or substitute words in the lines to create new or silly songs or poems.

Connections to the Standards

This book is designed to support you in meeting the following standards for grades K–1 as outlined by Mid-continent Research for Education and Learning (McREL), an organization that collects and synthesizes national and state standards.

Language Arts

Uses the general skills and strategies of the writing process
- uses drawings to express thoughts, feelings, and ideas
- uses writing and other methods (letters or phonetically spelled words, telling, dictating) to describe persons, places, objects, or experiences
- writes in a variety of forms or genres (picture books, letters, information pieces, messages, response to literature)

Uses grammatical and mechanical conventions in written compositions
- uses knowledge of letter-sound relationships to write simple words
- uses conventions of spelling in writing (spells level-appropriate high frequency and phonetically regular words)
- uses conventions of print in writing (uses uppercase and lowercase letters, spaces words, writes from left-to-right and top-to-bottom)
- knows that there are rules for forming sentences

Uses the general skills and strategies of the reading process
- uses meaning clues (picture captions, title, cover, story structure, topic) to aid comprehension and make predictions about content
- uses basic elements of phonetic analysis (letter-sound relationships, vowel sounds, blends, word patterns) to decode unknown words
- understands level-appropriate sight words and vocabulary

Uses reading skills and strategies to understand and interpret a variety of informational texts
- uses reading skills and strategies to understand a variety of informational texts (written directions, signs, captions, labels, informational books)
- understands the main idea and supporting details of simple expository information
- summarizes information found in text (retells in own words)
- relates new information to prior knowledge and experience

Uses listening and speaking strategies for different purposes
- uses new vocabulary, level-appropriate vocabulary, and descriptive language
- listens for a variety of purposes
- follows one- and two-step directions
- contributes to group discussions and follows the rules of conversation
- asks and responds to questions
- recites and responds to familiar songs, poems, and rhymes

History

Understands family life now and in the past, and family life in various places long ago
- knows the cultural similarities and differences in clothes, homes, food, communication, and cultural traditions between families now and in the past
- understands personal family or cultural heritage through stories, songs, and celebrations
- knows ways in which people share family beliefs and values (oral traditions, literature, songs, religion, community celebrations, food, language)

Understands how democratic values came to be, and how they have been exemplified by people, events, and symbols
- knows colonist leaders who fought for independence from England (George Washington, John Hancock, Paul Revere)
- understands how individuals have worked to achieve liberty, equality, and to improve the lives of people from many groups (Rosa Parks, Cesar Chavez, Martin Luther King, Jr.)
- knows how different groups of people in the community have taken responsibility for the common good (police, fire department)
- understands the reasons that Americans celebrate certain national holidays
- knows the history of American symbols (the eagle, Liberty Bell, national flag)
- knows why important buildings, statues, and monuments are associated with national history

Understands selected attributes and historical developments of societies in America and other countries
- knows the holidays and ceremonies of different societies

Kendall, J. S. & Marzano, R. J. (2004). *Content knowledge: A compendium of standards and benchmarks for K–12 education.* Aurora, CO: Mid-continent Research for Education and Learning. Online database: http://www.mcrel.org/standards-benchmarks/

I'm Special!

Children recognize their own uniqueness
and their similarities to others.

I'm Special!
I am special through and through.
I can **read** and **write**
and **help my sister** , too!
Name: **Jose**

Facts to Share

No two people are exactly alike—not even twins! Every person is different, with unique abilities, needs, and desires. While differences make each individual interesting and special, all people are alike in some ways, too. For instance, everyone eats, sleeps, and has a family or other group to which they belong.

Introducing the Activity

Invite children to share something special about themselves, such as their favorite color, food, or outdoor or indoor activity. After discussing, invite them to create these self-portraits. Then use the finished projects for the extension activity (below). Later, you might bind the pages into a book titled, "I'm Special!" for the class to enjoy.

What to Do

1. Cut out the pattern.

2. Fill in details to make the person in the picture resemble yourself. Color the eyes the same color as your own eyes. Use craft materials to decorate your picture. For example, you might add yarn hair, craft-foam ears, and glitter to make a sparkly shirt.

3. Write (or dictate) your own responses to complete the sentence.

Extension Activity

To reinforce children's color knowledge, label each of four sentence strips with *blue*, *green*, *brown* or *black*. Arrange the strips to create four columns. Then invite children to sort their self-portraits under the strips according to eye color. Have them compare the results of the graph and then use the pictures to discuss how they are alike and different. Afterward, teach children the song "Different and the Same."

BOOK 📖 BREAK

Incredible You! 10 Ways to Let Your Greatness Shine Through by Wayne Dyer and Kristina Tracy (Hay House, 2005). Simple, uplifting rhymes encourage children to create their own happiness with simple, positive ideas.

It's Okay to Be Different by Todd Parr (Little, Brown Young Readers, 2004). This colorful and optimistic book focuses on acceptance and individuality, encouraging readers to do the same.

MATERIALS

For each child:
- self-portrait pattern (page 80)
- scissors
- crayons
- craft materials (construction paper scraps, yarn, craft foam, glitter glue, and so on)
- glue

Different and the Same

(to the tune of "Yankee Doodle")

We are alike in many ways—
We eat and work and play.
We go to school, and laugh and learn.
We live in the U. S. A.!

We're not alike in many ways—
Our skin, our hair, our names.
And it's okay to be this way,
Both different and the same.

We're alike, oh, yes indeed.
But we are different, too.
It's okay to be this way,
I'm me, and you are you!

What Do I Need?

Children help create a class book
featuring our three basic needs.

Facts to Share

Everyone has needs, no matter where they live or what language they
speak. The basic needs of all people include food, clothing, and shelter.

Introducing the Activity

Ask children to share ideas about the things they need to live and
grow. Lead them to conclude that everyone has three basic needs: food,
shelter, and clothing. Talk about different kinds of food, clothing, and
shelter that are used to meet needs in your community as well as in
other areas of the country and world. Then invite children to create
pages for a class flip book about needs.

What to Do

1. Draw a type of food on one sheet of 6- by 12-inch construction
paper. Write "Food" at the top. Then write (or dictate) the name
of the food.

2. Repeat step 1 for the remaining two sheets of paper, drawing an
article of clothing and writing "Clothing" on one page and drawing
a type of shelter with the label "Shelter" on the other page.

To make the class book:

1. Write the title "What Do I Need?" on one 12- by 18-inch sheet
of construction paper. Then laminate both sheets of construction
paper for durability.

2. Have children sort their pages by the three categories. Stack and
staple each set of pages along the long left side of the untitled
12- by 18-inch construction paper.

3. Top the pages with the cover page and staple in place. To read,
have children randomly turn the pages for each section to reveal
things that satisfy the three basic needs.

Extension Activity

Label index cards with "Food," "Clothing," and "Shelter" and put them
in a paper bag. Then sing "Our Basic Needs" with children. (You might
copy the song onto chart paper to display as you sing.) Each time you
sing the song, invite a child to draw a card from the bag, read the label,
and name an item that can meet that need.

BOOK 📖 BREAK

Needs and Wants by Susan Ring (Yellow Umbrella Books, 2003).
This book highlights things that people need as well as things they
might want.

MATERIALS

For each child:
- three 6- by 12-inch pieces of
  white construction paper
- crayons

For the class:
- two 12- by 18-inch sheets
  of construction paper (in a
  light color)
- marker
- stapler

Our Basic Needs

(to the tune of "This Old Man")

Our basic needs are the same,
Although we all have different names,
For we all need shelter, food, and
  clothing, too—
Basic needs for me and you.

We All Live Together

Jobs at Home

Children create booklets about household jobs done by them and their families.

Working Together at Home

by **Dan**

Facts to Share

No matter where children live or whom they live with—whether their parents, relatives, or friends—household tasks must be done. When children work together with others in their home, chores can be fun and get done quickly. In addition, children can feel a sense of accomplishment when their teamwork gets great results!

Introducing the Activity

Encourage children to share what kinds of chores they do at home. Discuss chores that are suitable for children to do independently and those that are better handled by an adult. Afterward, invite children to make these personalized booklets to share with the members of their household.

What to Do

1. Color and cut out the cover and booklet pages.

2. Sequence and stack the pages behind the cover. Staple along the left side.

3. Write your name on the cover. Draw a picture on each of pages 1–4 to show which household member or members do the job.

4. Draw a picture of a special household chore you do on page 5.

Extension Activity

Gather common items that are used for chores, such as a plastic dish, mini laundry basket, sponge, duster, and plastic trowel. Place the items in a large laundry basket. During group time, invite children to select items from the basket and name chores that can be performed with the items. On each child's turn, sing "Working Together." Have the child fill in the blanks with a chore that uses the selected item (such as *wash the dishes, do the laundry, wipe the counter, dust the dresser,* and *plant the garden*).

• • • • • • • • BOOK 📖 BREAK • • • • • • • •

Home Tools by Inez Snyder (Children's Press, 2002). Features tools used to do everyday chores at home.

Teamwork by Lisa Trumbauer (Yellow Umbrella Books, 2000). Family members work together as a team to accomplish a job.

• • • • • • MATERIALS • • • • • •

For each child:
■ booklet patterns (pages 81–82)
■ scissors
■ pencil
■ crayons

To share:
■ stapler

Working Together

(to the tune of "Short'nin' Bread")

People in a household work together.
They work together to get chores done.
People in a household work together.
They work together to get chores done.

They [name of chore]. They get it done.
Working together makes chores more fun!
They [name of chore]. They get it done.
Working together makes chores more fun!

Lend a Hand!

Children discover that everyone lends a hand in making a great classroom community.

Facts to Share

Just as children belong to their families at home, they also belong to another family—their classroom family. And, just as there are jobs to do at home, there are also jobs to do in the classroom. From watering plants and cleaning up centers to leading the line and feeding the class pets, classroom jobs come in many different forms!

Introducing the Activity

Work with children to generate a list of classroom jobs and discuss why these jobs are needed. Invite them to share what might happen if these jobs were not done. Then, to create a job board, cut out a supply of large fishbowls from white construction paper, write each class job at the bottom of a fishbowl, and laminate for durability. Set up the job board and then invite children to make handprint fish to use on it.

What to Do

1. Paint your hand with tempera paint. Keep your fingers together as you press your hand onto the construction paper to make a handprint fish. Let the paint dry.

2. Use the marker to write your name on your handprint fish. Draw an eye and other simple features on the fish. Then cut out the fish.

To use on the display:

1. Laminate the handprint fish for durability.

2. To assign daily or weekly jobs, place a different child's fish on each fishbowl. Place the remaining fish along the bottom and sides of the display.

Extension Activity

Place a clear plastic fishbowl and a pocket chart near your job board display. Write each child's name on a die-cut fish, laminate all the fish, and then place them in the fishbowl. To use, invite pairs or small groups to find the names on the fish that match the names of the current classroom job-holders displayed on the job board. Have them place those fish in the pocket chart.

MATERIALS

For each child:
- 9- by 12-inch white construction paper
- orange tempera paint
- paint brush
- black marker
- scissors

・・・・・・・ BOOK 📖 BREAK ・・・・・・・

Responsibility by Cynthia Roberts (Child's World, 2007). Readers learn about acting responsibly at school, on the playground, and at home.

Cooperation Quilt

Children work together to create a quilt display.

Name: **Jake**

Facts to Share

It's important to work together at school. Cooperation promotes friendship—and fun! Sharing, taking turns, and listening to each other are ways that children can demonstrate cooperation and accomplish things together.

Introducing the Activity

Bring in a quilt to display to children. Explain that a quilt begins with one square. Alone, that square has very little use. But when many squares are put together, they can make a quilt that has many uses. Encourage children to discuss ways in which their cooperation with others helps accomplish classroom goals, such as keeping the room neat and organized, completing assignments on time, and enjoying recess on the playground. Then invite children to design quilt squares to create a class quilt display.

What to Do

1. Cut out the quilt pattern.

2. Write your name on the line.

3. Draw a self-portrait in the middle of your quilt square. Create a colorful design on the borders.

To make the display:

1. Alternate children's quilt squares with the 7-inch squares of construction paper to create a quilt design. Staple the arrangement of squares to a bulletin board.

2. If desired, copy "Together We Get Things Done" onto colorful paper and add it to the display.

Extension Activity

Copy each line of "Together We Get Things Done" onto a separate sentence strip. Display the sentence strips in sequence in a pocket chart. Then invite children to follow along as you read the poem several times. During each reading emphasize the rhyming words *fun* and *done*. Afterward, encourage children to brainstorm other words that rhyme with these words.

・・・・・・・・・・・・・・・・ BOOK 📖 BREAK ・・・・・・・・・・・・・・・・

Cooperation by Janet Riehecky (Capstone Press, 2005). Explores important character traits and examples of people using good judgment.

MATERIALS

For each child:
- quilt pattern (page 83)
- scissors
- crayons

For the display:
- 7-inch squares of construction paper in a variety of colors
- stapler

Together We Get Things Done

We learn and work and play at school.
Cooperation makes it fun.
Listening, sharing, taking turns—
Together we get things done.

Our School Community

Children create a class booklet about the members of their school community.

Facts to Share

A school is a community of adults and children who work together to create a safe and pleasant environment for learning. Children, teachers, adult workers, volunteers, and even classroom pets all have important roles in a school community.

Introducing the Activity

Ask children to name people they see in their school and classroom on a regular basis. They might identify teachers, classmates, adult workers, volunteers, and even classroom pets! Explain that many different parties come together to form their school community. Then invite children to create pages to include in a class booklet about their school community.

What to Do

1. Cut out the booklet page. Then draw someone from your school community in the box on the school.

2. Write the name of the person (or pet) on the line to complete the sentence. Write your name on the back of the page.

3. Staple the 5- by 6-inch construction paper to the left side of the page where indicated to create a flap over the picture.

To make the class booklet:

1. To create a cover for the class booklet, write the title "Who's in Our School Community?" on one of the sheets of construction paper. Add a drawing of the school, if desired.

2. Stack student pages between the sheets of construction paper, placing the cover on top. Staple the pages together along the left side.

Extension Activity

Place items that represent different school workers in a large box labeled "Lost and Found." You might include a stethoscope (nurse), small broom (custodian), food tray (cafeteria worker), book (librarian) and so on. Show one item at a time and ask children to name a school worker who might have lost the item. Then sing "Who Works at School?" Fill in the blanks with the school worker's name and job.

MATERIALS

For each child:
- booklet page (page 84)
- scissors
- crayons
- 5- by 6-inch construction paper (any color)

For the class:
- stapler
- two 9- by 12-inch sheets of construction paper (in a light color)
- marker

Who Works at School?

(to the tune of "London Bridge")

[Worker's name] works at school,
Works at school, works at school.
[Worker's name] works at school.
He's (she's) our [job name].

BOOK 📖 BREAK

At School by Lisa Trumbauer (Capstone Press, 2001). Photos illustrate children going to school and working in their classroom community.

School in Many Cultures by Heather Adams(Capstone, 2008). Explores the similarities and differences in schools around the world.

Community Pride!

Children create posters showing ways they can make their community the best it can be!

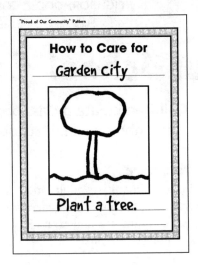

Facts to Share

It takes many hardworking citizens to create a community that everyone can be proud of. Following safety practices and rules, being kind and helpful to others, and keeping the community clean can bring a sense of pride to all community members.

Introducing the Activity

Discuss with children ways in which they might help make their community the best it can be. Encourage them to consider things they can do to help care for the people and places in their community, such as collecting canned goods for a food bank, visiting elderly citizens, and volunteering to plant flowers at a local park. Write children's suggestions on chart paper. Then invite them to create posters that highlight community care activities. Display the completed posters in your classroom.

What to Do

1. Write the name of your community on the line at the top of the poster.

2. Draw a picture of an activity you can do to show you care for the people or places in your community.

3. Write (or dictate) a description of the activity on the line at the bottom of the poster.

Extension Activity

Tell children that working together to beautify our neighborhoods is a great way to build community spirit and pride. Encourage children to name things citizens can do to beautify the community, such as grow flowers, clean up parks, paint buildings, and pick up trash. List their suggestions on a sheet of chart paper labeled with the heading "Keep [your community] Beautiful." To reinforce their ideas, sing "We Can Make Our Town Look Pretty." Each time you repeat the song, replace the underlined words with a different activity.

BOOK 📖 BREAK

The Gardening Book by Jane Bull (Dorling Kindersley, 2003). Child-friendly photos present gardening basics and easy outdoor projects.

Miss Lady Bird's Wildflowers: How a First Lady Changed America by Kathi Appelt (HarperCollins, 2005). Highlights Lady Bird Johnson's work in encouraging citizens to beautify roadways across America.

MATERIALS

For each child:
■ poster pattern (page 85)
■ crayons

We Can Make Our Town Look Pretty

(to the tune of "Have You Ever Seen a Lassie?")

We can make our town look pretty,
Look pretty, look pretty.
We can make our town look pretty,
So we can be proud.

Let's all work together
To make our town better.
We can all <u>grow flowers</u>,
So we can be proud.

We Love a Parade!

Children celebrate community parades
with these foldout booklets.

Facts to Share

On some special occasions, citizens show their community pride and
spirit by holding a parade. Some parades are large with marching
bands, colorful floats, and prancing horses. Others, such as small town
parades, might feature flag-carrying scouts, decorated cars and trucks,
candy-tossing clowns, and kids on bicycles!

Introducing the Activity

Ask children if they've ever watched or participated in a bike parade to
celebrate a special community event or holiday. Invite them to share
their experiences. Then have children give ideas about how they might
decorate wagons, bikes, and scooters for a parade. Afterward, have
them make these easy-to-read parade booklets.

What to Do

1. Cut out the booklet cover and pages. Glue the pages together
where indicated.

2. Color the cover and write your name on the line.

3. Color the pictures on pages 1–4. Use crayons, glitter glue, and
crinkle strips to add decorations to the pictures, such as balloons,
flags, and streamers.

4. Draw a picture of yourself in the parade on page 5.

5. Accordion-fold the pages of the booklet, making sure the cover is
on top.

Extension Activity

Help children create headbands to wear in a classroom parade. First,
have them write (or dictate) a word or phrase onto 3- by 25-inch strips
of light-colored bulletin board paper to describe their favorite part of a
parade. Next, have children decorate the strips by gluing colorful
die-cut paper shapes and glitter around their writing. Then fit the
decorated strips around their heads and staple the ends together.
Finally, invite children to wear their headbands as they parade around
the room to lively music.

● ● ● ● ● ● ● ● ● ● ● **BOOK 📖 BREAK** ● ● ● ● ● ● ● ● ● ● ●

Parade by Donald Crews (HarperTrophy, 1986). Bright colors and
simple text bring together all the components of a perfect parade.

● ● ● ● ● ● **MATERIALS** ● ● ● ● ● ●

For each child:
■ booklet patterns (pages 86–87)
■ scissors
■ glue stick
■ crayons

To share:
■ glitter glue
■ crinkle strips

Neighborhood Signs

Children identify common community
signs with this simple booklet.

**Signs
Around
the
Neighborhood**

by _Sasha_

Facts to Share

Communities contain more than just homes and schools. Some public
places that we all share include hospitals, libraries, post offices, and
parks. Special signs posted in communities help citizens identify these
important places.

Introducing the Activity

To introduce children to signs for public places in your community,
take digital photos of signs for the hospital, library, fire station, post
office, and so on. (Or color, cut out, and laminate the booklet sheets
on pages 88–89.) Display the photos in a pocket chart. Then have
children identify each sign, discussing any they might be unfamiliar
with. Afterward, invite them to make these booklets to reinforce their
sign identification.

MATERIALS

For each child:
■ booklet patterns (pages 88–89)
■ scissors
■ crayons

To share:
■ stapler

What to Do

1. Color and cut out the cover and booklet pages. Write your name
on the cover.

2. Sequence and stack the pages behind the cover. Staple them
together at the top left corner.

3. Use the color shown at the top right of each page to color the sign.

Community Chant

Restaurant, supermarket, clothing store, too.
These are places for me and you.
Police station, fire station, park, and school—
Places that make our neighborhood cool!
Hospital, post office, library—
Community places for you and me.

Extension Activity

Gather advertising circulars, brochures, and phone directory ads that
feature logos from local businesses such as banks, restaurants, and
clothing and grocery stores. Then have small groups cut out logos and
glue them to 12- by 18-inch sheets of construction paper to make
posters. Display the posters on a bulletin board titled "Around the
Community." Invite groups to read aloud the logos on their posters.
Wrap up the activity by teaching children the "Community Chant."

BOOK 📖 BREAK

On the Town: A Community Adventure by Judith Caseley
(Greenwillow, 2002). Mother and son run errands to different
places in their community.

Good Groceries!

Children make this shopping-bag booklet
to practice reading environmental print.

Facts to Share
Everyone needs food to live. Some people grow their own food, but
many people buy their food at grocery stores and supermarkets.

Introducing the Activity
Show children sales circulars from several grocery stores in your area.
Point out the store logos on the circulars and have children identify
the store. Then invite them to make shopping bag booklets to take
home and read with their families.

What to Do

1. Cut off the bottom of the paper bag along the bottom fold (the bag
will be 9 inches tall). Then cut off one side. Cut out a 3-inch square
from the removed side for later use.

2. For the booklet cover, fold the bag in half. Stack and fold the two
sheets of white paper in half. Fit the folded pages inside the cover
and staple along the fold.

3. Cut out the title and page patterns. Glue the title to the cover of
the booklet. Write your name on the line.

4. Glue the page pattern to the inside back cover. Then glue the
3-inch square to the page, where indicated, to create a pocket that
represents an open grocery bag.

5. Cut out five food items from the circulars. Glue a picture to each
blank page and write (or dictate) the name of the food.

6. Glue the last food cutout partially inside the grocery-bag pocket on
the back page. Write the name of the food on the blank to complete
the sentence.

⋯⋯⋯⋯ **MATERIALS** ⋯⋯⋯⋯

For each child:
■ title and page patterns
  (page 90)
■ brown paper lunch bag
■ two 8½- by 11-inch sheets of
  white paper
■ scissors
■ glue
■ pencil

To share:
■ stapler
■ local grocery store circulars

Extension Activity
To reinforce children's logo recognition skills, cut out store logos from
sales circulars for stores in your area. Glue each logo to an index card
and display the cards in the top row of a pocket chart. To use, have
children place cards labeled with their names under the logo for the store
they visit most often. When finished, review and discuss the graph results.

⋯⋯⋯⋯ BOOK 📖 BREAK ⋯⋯⋯⋯

Signs at the Store by Mary Hill (Children's Press, 2003). Photo-
illustrations feature a girl and her father shopping at the grocery store.

A Visit to the Supermarket by B. A. Hoena (Pebble Plus, 2004). This
book profiles a supermarket, its workers, and various departments in
the store.

Eating Out

Children read menus and take orders as they role-play restaurant dining experiences.

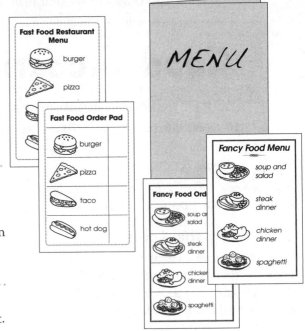

Facts to Share

There are many kinds of restaurants, from fast food establishments where customers seat and serve themselves to casual diners that offer table service and grilled-to-order foods to formal restaurants that provide sophisticated service and gourmet dishes. Restaurants are often staffed with cooks, servers, cashiers, dishwashers, and more.

Introducing the Activity

Describe fast food and fine-dining restaurants. Invite children to tell about and compare their dining experiences at each kind of restaurant. Then hold a Fast Food Day and a Fancy Food Day on separate days.

What to Do

Set up each type of restaurant. Then invite children to role-play cooks, servers, cashiers, customers, and so on. Have them use the order pads to record customer orders.

Setting up the fast food restaurant:

1. Collect unused containers from local fast-food restaurants (pizza boxes, french-fry boxes, take-out bags, and so on). Also, gather paper plates, cups, and napkins.

2. Enlarge and laminate a copy of the menu on page 91. Copy a supply of the order pad.

3. Arrange the center and props to resemble a fast food restaurant. Post the enlarged menu on a wall behind the "counter" for customers to view.

Setting up the fancy food restaurant:

1. Gather tablecloths, cloth napkins, empty salt and pepper shakers, stem vases with artificial flowers, and plastic plates, bowls, and cups.

2. Copy and cut out several copies of the menu on page 92. Also, copy a supply of the order pad. For each menu, fold a sheet of 9- by 12-inch construction paper in half card-style and glue the menu on the inside. Write "Menu" on the outside.

3. Arrange the center and props to resemble a fancy restaurant with tablecloths on the tables, flower centerpieces, place settings and menus at each seat, and so on.

MATERIALS

For both centers:
- order pads and menus (pages 91–92)
- toy cash register
- plastic foods and eating utensils
- play money
- aprons
- play kitchen equipment
- pencils

For more materials, see Setting up the restaurants *(at left).*

BOOK 📖 BREAK

Chef Ki Is Serving Dinner! by Jill D. Duvall (Children's Press, 1997). Features a behind-the-scenes visit with Chef Ki and his wife at their neighborhood restaurant in Virginia.

Fast Food Restaurant by Lois M. Schaeffer (Heinemann Library, 2001). A simple introduction to who works at a fast food restaurant.

Library Basics

Children sequence the steps to follow
to borrow items from the library.

I choose
a ___book___.

I check out
the ___book___.

I take the
___book___ home.

I return the
___book___ to the library.

Facts to Share

Libraries are important places where people gather to read, learn, use
computers, attend community events, and borrow books, movies, music
materials, and other types of media.

Introducing the Activity

Invite children to describe the steps to follow when borrowing a book,
magazine, videotape, or DVD from the library. Don't forget to include
the important final step—returning the item to the library on time!
Then recite "Borrowing a Book" with children to reinforce the check-
out process. Afterward, have them create and sequence this set of cards
to show their understanding of how borrowing from a library works.

What to Do

1. Cut out the cards. Read each card and decide what item you might
check out from the library, such as a book, magazine, or CD.
Complete the sentence on each card by writing (or dictating) the
name of the item on the line.

2. Sequence the cards to show the steps for checking out the item.
Then draw a picture to represent each step.

3. Write a numeral from 1–4 in the box at the top right of each card.

4. Glue the cards in the correct order onto the sheet of construction
paper.

Extension Activity

Invite children to make a class book about a librarian's job. First,
have children draw pictures of librarians performing their jobs on
9- by 12-inch sheets of white paper. Then ask them to write (or dictate)
sentences to describe their pictures. Staple the completed pages
together between construction paper covers and title the book
"A Librarian's Job." Then invite children to check out the book from
your classroom library.

BOOK 📖 BREAK

That's Our Librarian! by Ann Morris (Millbrook Press, 2003).
This photo-illustrated book introduces children to an elementary
school librarian.

Welcome to the Library by Alyse Sweeney (Children's Press, 2006).
Text and photos follow a librarian as she performs an important
community job.

MATERIALS

For each child:
- library sequencing cards
  (page 93)
- scissors
- crayons
- 12- by 18-inch sheet of
  construction paper
- glue

Borrowing a Book

I go to the library and look on each shelf.
I decide on a book that I pick out myself!
I walk to the counter. I go quietly.
The librarian checks the book out to me.
I take the book home—read it three times
    or four!
Then I take the book back to the library
    once more.

A Place for Fun

Children help create a class booklet filled with their favorite community recreational places.

When I need a relaxing day,
I like to go to ___the park___
for fun or play!

by ___Kara___

Facts to Share

Communities provide more than just places to work—they also include places designed for fun, relaxation, and recreation. Individuals and families might visit a local park, zoo, lake, theater, shopping center, or other facility that allows them to relax and enjoy their leisure time.

Introducing the Activity

Talk with children about places in the community that they might visit for recreation and relaxation. Invite them to share about their favorite leisure time activities such as riding bikes, visiting the zoo, or going to a movie. Then have children create pages to use in a class guide about the recreational places in their community. Invite them to take turns taking the guide home to share with their families.

What to Do

1. To complete the sentence, write (or dictate) the name of a place in your community that you like to go to for recreation—either by yourself, with friends, or with your family.

2. Draw a picture to illustrate the sentence.

3. Write your name on the line at the bottom of the page.

To make the class booklet:

1. To create a cover for the class booklet, write the title "Our Community Recreation Guide" on one of the sheets of construction paper. Add a drawing of the community, if desired.

2. Stack student pages together between the sheets of construction paper, placing the cover on top. Staple the pages together along the left side.

Extension Activity

To help children classify local recreational places, cut a large building shape from white bulletin board paper and title it "Indoor Recreation." Then cut a large shrub shape from green bulletin board paper and title it "Outdoor Recreation." Have children brainstorm local indoor and outdoor recreational sites to list on the appropriate shapes. Afterward, sing "Recreation" with the class.

MATERIALS

For each child:
■ booklet page (page 94)
■ crayons
■ pencil

For the class:
■ two 9- by 12-inch sheets of construction paper (in a light color)
■ marker
■ stapler

Recreation

(to the tune of "Clementine")

Recreation, recreation, here in our community.
Means good times in special places—so much fun for you and me.

Recreation, recreation—play a sport or ride a bike.
Take a walk, go roller skating, take a swim or take a hike.

Recreation, recreation—see a play, visit the zoo.
Go to a concert, watch a movie—so many fun things we can do!

BOOK 📖 BREAK

Let's Go to a Baseball Game, Let's Go to a Park, and *Let's Go to a Play* by Mary Hill (Children's Press, 2004). This series features books about great recreation places.

A Trip to the Zoo by Mae Sue Leslie (Providence Publishing, 2002). Beautiful illustrations fill this story about a family's day at the zoo.

Doctor, Doctor!

Children make this booklet about a visit to the doctor.

Facts to Share

Doctors take care of people who are sick or hurt, and they also help keep healthy people well. During a health examination, a doctor usually checks the patient's heartbeat, eyes, ears, and nose. The doctor may also do other things, such as take the patient's temperature and blood pressure.

Introducing the Activity

Hold a discussion about doctors with children. Ask questions such as "What do doctors do?" "What do they wear at work?" and "What instruments do they use?" Invite children to tell about their experiences with doctors, encouraging the group to listen and respond. Then have them make these mini-booklets that feature a few things they can expect when visiting a doctor. Encourage children to take their booklets home to share with family and friends.

What to Do

1. Cut out the booklet backing and pages.

2. Sequence the pages and stack them behind the stethoscope cover. Attach the pages to the backing by stapling along the left side of the pages.

3. Write your name on the line under the stethoscope.

4. Read each page and then draw a picture to illustrate the text.

Extension Activity

Show children examples of how quotation marks are used in picture books, explaining that they set off a speaker's words. Then invite children to write (or dictate) a quote of their own. At the top of a sheet of paper, write: *When the doctor* _____, *I say, "*_____.*"* Give copies to children and have them complete the sentence, filling in the first blank with something a doctor might do and the second blank with something they might say in response (for example, *When the doctor gives me a shot, I say, "That feels like a bee sting"*). Ask children to illustrate their sentences, then share their work with the class.

● ● ● ● ● ● ● ● ● ● ● ● **BOOK 📖 BREAK** ● ● ● ● ● ● ● ● ● ● ● ●

ABC Doctor by Liz Murphy (Blue Apple, 2007). The ABCs of visiting a doctor are depicted in colorful, collage illustrations.

● ● ● ● **MATERIALS** ● ● ● ●

For each child:
■ booklet patterns
  (pages 95–96)
■ crayons

To share:
■ stapler

Open Wide!

Children learn about dentists and caring for
their teeth with this lift-the-flap picture.

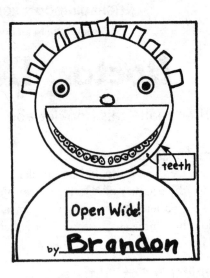

Facts to Share

People visit the dentist to keep their teeth healthy. While there, they
might get their teeth cleaned or seek treatment for a toothache.
Between visits, dentists advise patients to brush and floss their teeth at
least twice a day to remove food and germs and help prevent cavities.

Introducing the Activity

Discuss a visit to the dentist, asking questions such as "What does a
dentist do? "What tools does the dentist use?" and "How can you help
the dentist?" Then show children a toothbrush, toothpaste, dental floss,
and mouthwash. Explain that the dentist often tells patients to use
these things to help keep their teeth healthy. After reviewing healthy
dental habits, invite children to look inside their mouths—using
hand-held mirrors—to identify their teeth, tongue, and roof of mouth.
Then invite them to make these lift-the-flap pictures that they can use
to describe ways to practice healthy dental care.

MATERIALS

For each child:
- picture page and patterns
  (pages 97–98)
- scissors
- crayons
- glue
- two wiggle eyes

What to Do

1. Cut out and color the mouth pattern. Fold it in half with the
   colored sides folded together.

2. Glue the bottom half of the mouth where indicated on the picture
   page. Leave the top half of the mouth free to open and close.

3. Cut out the title and word patterns. Glue each one to the
   appropriate box on the picture and in the mouth.

4. Close the mouth. Glue wiggle eyes to the face. Draw other facial
   features on the picture so that it resembles you. Then color the
   rest of the picture.

Dentist Talk

Open wide, I'll check inside
To find the places plaque can hide.

Tooth that's new? Good for you!
Now I'll check the rest out, too.

I'm glad to say you're cavity-free.
Your teeth are as healthy as can be!

Extension Activity

Copy "Dentist Talk" onto chart paper. Explain that this poem is written
from the dentist's point of view. Then read the poem with children
several times and have them find the rhyming patterns. Can they think
of other words that rhyme with the rhyming pairs in the poem?

BOOK 📖 BREAK

Dentists by Dee Ready (Bridgestone Books, 1998). Photos and
simple text examine dentists' work, tools, clothing, and schooling.

Police on the Go

Children create this booklet about different forms
of transportation used by police officers.

Facts to Share

Police officers use various modes of transportation in their jobs. Some
use patrol cars or motorcycles to do their jobs, while others patrol
areas on foot or bicycles. Mounted police ride horses and often are
used for crowd patrol. Harbor police travel by water and help patrol
oceans, rivers, and large lakes. Some officers use helicopters, especially
when searching large or busy areas.

Introducing the Activity

Show children pictures of different kinds of police vehicles. (You might
use pictures from the books listed in "Book Break.") Discuss the
particular jobs that police officers perform using each vehicle. For
example, they use boats to patrol waterways and bicycles to patrol busy
city streets and areas that are hard for a car to reach. Afterward, invite
children to create these booklets about police transportation.

What to Do

1. Cut out the title and picture patterns (page 98). Glue each one to
the corresponding box on the booklet cover and pages. Write your
name on the line on the cover.

2. Color the picture on the cover and each page.

3. Cut out the cover and pages. Sequence the pages behind the cover
and staple them together along the left edge.

Extension Activity

Copy "Always on the Go!" onto chart paper. Ask children to name
different ways police officers travel to do their jobs. List their responses
on the chalkboard. Then teach children the song. Fill in the blanks
with one way a police officer might travel, phrasing the words from the
officer's perspective (for example, "I've been driving my police car,
working every day"). Each time you repeat the song, invite a different
child to fill in the blanks. Children might fill in the blanks with
"walking on the sidewalks," "riding on my bicycle," or "flying in
my helicopter."

MATERIALS

For each child:
- booklet patterns
  (pages 98–101)
- scissors
- glue
- crayons

To share:
- stapler

Always on the Go!

*(to the tune of "I've Been Working
on the Railroad")*

I've been [form of transportation], working
  every day.
I've been [form of transportation], just to keep
  you safe today.
I protect your streets and houses, and help
  the traffic flow,
'Cause I've been [form of transportation],
  I'm always on the go!

BOOK 📖 BREAK

A Day in the Life of a Police Officer by Mary Bowman-Kruhm
(Powerkids Press, 2001). Join a police officer and his dog on patrol.

I'm Going to Be a Police Officer by Edith Kundalt (Sagebrush
Education Resources, 2001). Simple text and clear, bright photos
combine to describe the duties of a police officer.

Fire Trucks at Work

Children spark an interest in firefighters
and their jobs with this interactive fire truck.

Facts to Share

Firefighters rely on many types of equipment to do their job. Fire
trucks are equipped with horns, lights, and sirens to warn others when
firefighters must get to fires quickly and safely. These important
vehicles also carry hoses, ladders, and many tools that firefighters
need for their work.

Introducing the Activity

Read *All Aboard Fire Trucks* by Teddy Slater. Talk with children about
the different kinds of equipment on fire trucks, how they are used, and
why they are important. Then invite children to make these fire trucks
with moveable parts. To use, have them lift the flaps, turn the wheels,
and read the labels for the different parts of the truck.

What to Do

1. Color and cut out the fire truck patterns.

2. Fold the window flap in half and glue the two sides together. Glue
the flap to the fire truck so that the word *firefighter* is on the inside
of the flap.

3. Glue the door flap and ladder to the truck where indicated.
Fold the ladder down and behind the truck.

4. Use a paper brad to attach the light wheel to the top of the truck
where indicated. Then attach the siren wheel to the front of the
truck with a paper brad.

Extension Activity

Sing "The Fire Truck Song" with children, inviting them to use their
movable trucks to act out the words. Each time they repeat the song,
have them sing one of the following:

The fire truck siren goes *whoo, whoo, whoo.*
The ladder on the truck goes up and down.
The firefighter says, "I'm here to help!"
The firefighter says, "Please, pass my gloves!"
The firefighter says, "Turn on the hose!"
The firefighter says, "I'll use the ax!"

MATERIALS

For each child:
- fire truck patterns
  (pages 102–103)
- crayons
- scissors
- glue stick
- 2 paper brads

The Fire Truck Song

(to the tune of "The Wheels on the Bus")

The fire truck lights go flash-flash-flash,
Flash-flash-flash, flash-flash-flash.
The fire truck lights go flash-flash-flash,
All through the town.

BOOK 📖 BREAK

All Aboard Fire Trucks by Teddy Slater (Grosset & Dunlap, 1991).
This picture book features the fire trucks and other equipment firefighters use.

Firefighters A to Z by Chris L. Demarest (Margaret K. McElderry,
2000). Large format, rhyming text, and action-packed illustrations
feature firefighters and their jobs.

Our Post Office

Children explore jobs at the post office with the help of these personalized mailboxes.

Facts to Share

The many different jobs at the post office make it possible for postal workers to deliver mail to every residence and business in every city, suburb, town, and village in our country. Each letter carrier delivers an average of 2,900 pieces of mail every day!

Introducing the Activity

Invite children to share what they know about how mail is delivered. Then share one of the books listed in "Book Break"—or another book of your choice—to review the different jobs performed by postal workers. While reading, pause to discuss each job and let children share their personal knowledge of the job. Afterward, have children create these personalized mailboxes. Display the mailboxes on a bulletin board titled "You've Got Mail!" Encourage children to write and deliver letters to their classmates' mailboxes.

What to Do

1. Color and cut out the mailbox and lid patterns.

2. Glue the mailbox near the bottom of the construction paper. Glue down only the bottom and sides of the mailbox, leaving the top end open to create a pocket.

3. Position the lid above the mailbox so that its bottom edge overlaps the top edge of the mailbox. Glue the lid in place only along the top edge to create a flap.

4. Write your name and your teacher's name on the lines on the mailbox where indicated.

Extension Activity

Place bulk mail letters, magazines, store flyers, and small packages in a large plastic bin. Then create a label for each of type of mail represented: letters, magazines, store ads, and packages. Attach each label to a separate small bin and help children read the labels. Next, have children sort the mail into the appropriate small bins. Conclude by singing "Post Office Sorting." Each time children repeat the song, have them replace *letters* with *magazines*, *store ads*, or *packages*.

BOOK 📖 BREAK

Postal Workers by Cynthia Fitterer Klingel (Child's World, 2001). Photo-illustrations show all the workers needed to deliver mail to our door.

Postal Workers by Shannon Knudsen (Lerner Publications, 2005). This book features workers who sort mail, sell stamps, drive trucks, and deliver mail.

MATERIALS

For each child:
- mailbox and lid patterns (page 104)
- 9- by 12-inch sheet of construction paper (any color)
- scissors
- crayons
- glue stick

Post Office Sorting

(to the tune of "Ten Little Indians")

Work at the post office, sort all the **letters**.
Work at the post office, sort all the **letters**.
Work at the post office, sort all the **letters**.
Then send all the mail along its way!

It's Trash Day!

Children learn how they can help sanitation workers separate recyclables from trash.

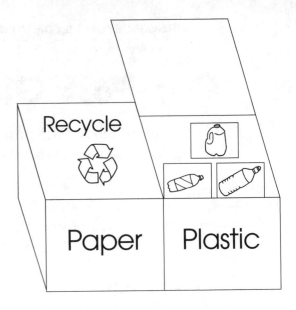

Facts to Share ....

Sanitation workers work for the community, collecting trash and recyclables. They provide a service, making sure that unwanted trash and recyclable items are properly disposed of.

Introducing the Activity ....

Place recyclable plastic and paper items in a large grocery bag. During group time, empty the bag and ask children if they put any of these things in their trashcans. Explain that all the items can be recycled. Then sort the paper items from the plastic ones. Tell children that they can help sanitation workers (and the community) by separating recyclables from trash. Finally, invite children to make these lift-the-flap recycle bins.

What to Do ....

1. Color and cut out the recycle bin, lids, and pictures of recyclable items. Color the bin and lids the same color.

2. Glue a lid to the top of each side of the recycle bin, gluing only along the top edge to create a flap.

3. Sort the pictures by the type of material each item is made of: paper or plastic.

4. Open the flap on each side of the bin. Glue the pictures of the paper items on the left side of the bin and the plastic items on the right. Close the lids.

Extension Activity ....

To reinforce recycling, place plastic and paper recyclable items in a large box. Label each of two laundry baskets "Plastic" or "Paper." Then give each child a turn to remove an item from the box and place it in the appropriate basket for recycling. At the end of each child's turn, chant "Who Recycles?" to the rhythm of "Who Took the Cookies From the Cookie Jar?" Use the name of the item and the child's name to fill in the blanks. Invite the child to give a solo response in the third and fifth lines of the chant.

> ● ● ● ● ● ● **BOOK 📖 BREAK** ● ● ● ● ● ● ● ● ●
>
> *Garbage Collectors* by Paulette Bourgeois (Kids Can Press, 2001). Readers learn how garbage is separated for recycling, taken to a transfer station, and compacted for storage in landfills.
>
> *Where Does the Garbage Go?* by Paul Showers (Harper Trophy, 1994). How do we deal with trash? Follow the garbage truck to the landfill and find out.

● ● ● ● ● **MATERIALS** ● ● ● ● ●

For each child:
- recycle bin patterns and pictures (pages 105–106)
- crayons
- scissors
- glue

Who Recycles?

Who put the [name of item] in the recycle bin?
[Name of child] put the [name of item] in the
 recycle bin.
Who me?
Yes, you.
I did!
Good for you!

Whose Tool?

Children read the names of tools used by community workers to build word recognition skills.

Facts to Share

Community workers use many different kinds of tools. Some may even use the same kind of tools! For instance, firefighters and gardeners use hoses, and artists and house painters use paintbrushes.

Introducing the Activity

Gather a variety of tools used by community workers (such as a hammer, hairbrush, stethoscope, wire whisk, dental floss, brick, paintbrush, and book). Ask children to identify each tool and name community workers who might use it in their occupation. Then help build children's word recognition skills with this activity.

What to Do

1. Write the name of each tool and a community worker who uses the tool on separate index cards. Stack the tool cards facedown and spread out the worker cards face up.

2. Place the tools in a box. Invite a child to take the top card from the stack, read the tool name, and find that tool in the box.

3. Ask the child to find the card for the worker who uses the tool.

4. Have the child place the tool and worker cards together in the pocket chart. Then ask the group if they agree that the cards make a match. If so, leave the cards in the chart. If not, help the child find a correct worker card to place in the chart.

5. Continue until every child has had a turn or all the cards have been correctly paired.

Extension Activity

Write the name of community workers and their workplaces on separate index cards (such as *teacher/school, doctor/hospital, librarian/library, firefighter/fire station,* and *mechanic/gas station*). Have small groups match the worker and workplace cards and display the pairs in a pocket chart. Then sing "Who Works There?" Fill in the blank with a workplace, pointing to the corresponding card as you sing. Have children answer the last question in the song with the name of the worker.

MATERIALS

- variety of tools used by community workers
- large box
- 4- by 6-inch index cards
- marker
- pocket chart

Who Works There?

(to the tune of "Mary Wore a Red Dress")

Who works at a [workplace], [workplace], [workplace]?
Who works at a [workplace]? Do you know?

BOOK 📖 BREAK

Whose Tools Are These?: A Look at Tools Workers Use—Big, Sharp, and Smooth by Sharon Katz Cooper (Picture Window Books, 2007). A look at the special tools used by various workers, including a chef, teacher, and hairdresser.

Just Passing By

Children take a survey of the land
vehicles that travel around their school.

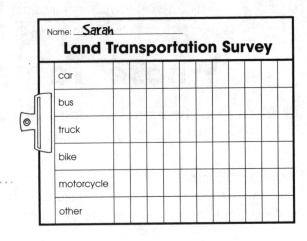

Name: Sarah								
Land Transportation Survey								
car								
bus								
truck								
bike								
motorcycle								
other								

Facts to Share

Vehicles that travel on land move people and products around the
community. Land vehicles come in all shapes and sizes, and many—
but not all (such as horses, sleds, and skis)—have wheels .

Introducing the Activity

Invite children to brainstorm the kinds of land vehicles that might
travel by the school. List their responses on chart paper. Then ask
them to predict which of the listed vehicles they might see pass by
most frequently. Afterward, take children to an area where they can
safely watch vehicles pass by. Give them five to ten minutes to conduct
these surveys. Then have them use the results to check their guesses.

What to Do

1. Write your name on the survey. Staple the survey to the cardboard.

2. Go to a safe area to watch vehicles. On the signal to begin, use a
pencil to draw an X in a box next to each type of vehicle you see.
Work from left to right across each row. Continue until signaled
to stop.

3. Back in the classroom, choose a different color for each kind of
vehicle on the chart. Color all the boxes marked with an X in each
row with the color for that vehicle.

4. Share and compare the results of your graph with classmates.
What kind of vehicle travels by your school most frequently?

Extension Activity

Create a display about children's favorite ways to travel around the
community. To begin, ask children to draw their favorite land vehicle
on the left side of a sheet of paper and a place in their community on
the right side. Then have them write (or dictate) "This [name of
vehicle] is going to [name of destination]." across the top. Display the
pages, along with a local map, on a bulletin board titled "Traveling in
Our Town."

MATERIALS

For each child:
■ survey chart (page 107)
■ 9- by 12-inch piece of
corrugated cardboard
■ pencil
■ crayon

To share:
■ stapler

BOOK 📖 BREAK

Traveling on Land by Deborah Chancellor (Two-Can Publishers,
2000). Full-color photos are featured in this book about
land transportation.

Wheels Around by Shelley Rotner (Houghton Mifflin, 1995). All
kinds of wheeled people and product movers appear in this photo-
illustrated book.

Rules of the Road

Children learn to read signs and symbols
with this unique road signs booklet.

Facts to Share ....

Road signs come in a variety of shapes and colors and contain words
or symbols to communicate their messages. Without road signs, the
traffic on our roads would be chaotic and unpredictable.

Introducing the Activity ....

To introduce road signs, color, laminate, and cut out enlarged copies of
the road sign patterns on pages 108–109. (Use the colors that are on
actual road signs.) Place the signs in a pocket chart. Then explain
that road signs communicate rules of the road and other important
information. Point to one sign at a time and have children "read" it
and discuss its meaning. If the sign has a symbol, talk about why that
symbol is used. Finally, have children make these booklets to share
their road sign knowledge. (Display the sign cards in the pocket chart
for children to use as a color guide.)

What to Do ....

1. Color the cover and write your name on the line.

2. Color the signs on each booklet page the color indicated below,
using displayed pictures of the signs as a coloring guide.

Red
page 2: Yield
page 4: Do Not Enter
page 6: No Parking
page 10: Stop

Green
page 8: Bike Route

Yellow
page 3: Railroad Crossing
page 7: School Crossing

Blue
page 5: Handicapped
Parking

3. Leave the signs on booklet pages 1 and 9 white. Color the signpost
at the bottom of page 10 black.

4. Use the pencil to trace the letters and words on the signs that
contain them.

5. Cut out the booklet cover and pages. Sequence the pages behind
the cover, with page 10 serving as the booklet backing. Staple the
booklet together along the top edge.

BOOK 📖 BREAK

I Read Signs by Tana Hoban (HarperTrophy, 1987). Striking photos
introduce readers to signs and symbols seen along roadways.

Red Light, Green Light by Anastasia Suen (Gulliver Books, 2005).
A boy plays with toy vehicles and action figures.

MATERIALS

For each child:
- booklet patterns
  (pages 108–109)
- crayons
- pencil
- scissors

To share:
- stapler

Go, Boat, Go!

Children set a course for reading success
with this water travel booklet.

Facts to Share

Boats are used for travel all over the world. Whether a small boat making local trips or a big freighter crossing the ocean, boats navigate rivers, lakes, and seas to move people and products from place to place.

Introducing the Activity

Introduce the topic of boats by sharing one or both of the books listed in "Book Break." Then discuss the different boats featured in the book(s), as well as any other kinds of boats children might be familiar with. To conclude, invite children to make these booklets that feature boats on the move.

What to Do

1. Use the blue marker to draw waves on the dark blue construction paper. Then color the entire page with the light blue crayon to create a wavy water scene. This page will be the backing of your booklet.

2. Cut out, sequence, and stack the booklet cover and pages. Center the stack of pages along the bottom edge of the water scene backing. Staple along the left side of the pages to attach them to the backing.

3. Write your name on the cover. Then draw a picture on each page to illustrate the sentence and color the water. On page 5, draw two or more kinds of boats.

4. Cut shapes from construction paper scraps to make a simple boat. Glue the boat to the booklet backing above the pages so that it appears to be floating on water.

Extension Activity

Have children name the different boats featured in their booklets. List the boats on chart paper. Then ask children to brainstorm other kinds of boats, such as cruise ships, steamboats, ferries, and tugboats to add to the list. Afterward, sing "My Boat Goes Over the Ocean." Each time you repeat the song, invite a child to name a boat from the list to replace *rowboat*.

BOOK 📖 BREAK

Busy Boats by Tony Mitton (Kingfisher, 2005). Colorful characters board a variety of vessels from a zippy little motorboat to a colossal cruise ship.

Harbor by Donald Crews (HarperTrophy, 1987). A fleet of colorful boats bustle about a very busy harbor.

MATERIALS

For each child:
- booklet patterns (pages 110–111)
- 6- by 9-inch sheet of dark blue construction paper
- light blue crayon
- crayons
- construction paper scraps
- glue stick

To share:
- stapler

My Boat Goes Over the Ocean

(to the tune of "My Bonnie Lies Over the Ocean")

My **rowboat** goes over the ocean.
My **rowboat** goes over the sea.
My **rowboat** goes over the ocean.
It takes me where I want to be!

Go, boat! Go, boat!
My **rowboat** goes over the sea, the sea.
Go, boat! Go, boat!
My **rowboat** goes over the sea!

What Can Fly?

Children learn about flying vehicles
with this easy-to-make booklet.

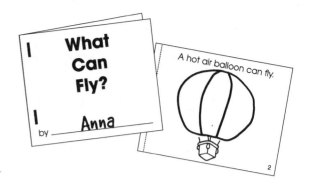

Facts to Share

The first manned flight was in a hot air balloon. Later, Orville and
Wilbur Wright built and flew the first successful airplane. Instead of
wings, helicopters have blades—or rotors—that help them fly through
the air or hover above the ground.

Introducing the Activity

To introduce air vehicles, challenge children to solve this riddle:

> I'm thinking of a vehicle. Tell me if you know.
> It has many seats and can travel fast or slow.
> It carries lots of people—there's luggage everywhere.
> It speeds down a runway, then flies into the air.

After children conclude that the riddle is about an airplane, encourage
them to brainstorm other flying vehicles (helicopters, blimps, rockets,
the space shuttle, and so on). Then have them make these booklets
about vehicles that fly. If desired, they might add pages for other kinds
of flying vehicles.

What to Do

1. Cut out, sequence, and stack the cover and pages. Staple the
   booklet together along the left side.

2. Write your name on the line on the cover.

3. Add wings to the airplane on page 1 and color the picture.

4. Draw a hot-air balloon on page 2, connecting it to the basket at
   the bottom of the page. Color the picture.

5. Draw a rotor on the helicopter and color the picture.

Extension Activity

Explain that helicopters are called whirlybirds because their rotors
whirl around as they fly. Tell children that helicopters can fly forward,
sideways, backwards, and hover in one place. Then share "I'm a
Whirlybird" with them. You might copy the poem onto chart paper
and have children read along as you recite it. When they become
familiar with the poem, invite children to invent movements to go
along with the words.

BOOK 📖 BREAK

I Love Planes! by Philemon Sturges (HarperCollins, 2003). Describes
jobs of many kinds of airplanes from biplanes and gliders to
seaplanes and dive-bombers.

MATERIALS

For each child:
- booklet patterns (page 112)
- scissors
- crayons

To share:
- stapler

I'm a Whirlybird

I'm a whirlybird. I fly through the air.
I can fly most anywhere.

Hop on passengers. Get buckled in!
I'll start my rotor. Watch it spin, spin, spin.

I'm a whirlybird, ready to fly.
Then I lift off and zoom through the sky.

I fly to the left, go backward, and right.
Then I stop and hover with all my might.

I'm a whirlybird, flying through the air.
I can fly most anywhere!

Transportation Everywhere!

Children identify different modes of transportation with this foldout booklet.

Facts to Share

Vehicles can travel almost everywhere: on land, on water, and in the air. Many have special parts or equipment that help them move. For example, some land vehicles have pedals or blades (ice skates, sleds), some air vehicles have wings and/or propellers, and some boats have sails or paddles.

Introducing the Activity

Label three separate sheets of chart paper with "Land," "Water," or "Air." Then invite children to take turns naming a vehicle. Have the class decide whether that vehicle travels on land, water, or in the air. Write the name of the vehicle on the chart that corresponds to children's decision. Afterward, have children make these booklets about land, water, and air vehicles.

What to Do

1. Draw a vehicle that travels by land on page 1, by water on page 2, and by air on page 3. Color the picture on each page.

2. Write your name on the line on page 4.

3. Cut out the pages. Glue pages 2 and 3 together where indicated.

4. Fold page 1 over page 2 and then page 3. Fold page 4 back so that it serves as the cover. To read, unfold the entire booklet and begin reading on page 1.

Extension Activity

Using the charts in "Introducing the Activity," choose and write the names of several vehicles on separate large index cards. Distribute the cards to children and have them illustrate the named vehicles on the back of their cards. When finished, help children sort the vehicles by different attributes, such as number of wheels, engine or no engine, number of passengers, or use (business, personal, recreation). Later, sing "On the Go" with children. To generate new verses for the song, have children replace *car* with vehicles named on their cards.

BOOK 📖 BREAK

Transportation by Margaret C. Hall (Heinemann, 2001). A look at various modes of transportation used throughout the world.

Transportation Then and Now by Robin Nelson (Lerner Publications, 2003). Readers learn about how transportation has changed over time.

MATERIALS

For each child:
■ booklet pages (page 113)
■ crayons
■ pencil
■ glue stick

On the Go

(to the tune of "The Farmer in the Dell")

The **car** is on the go.
The **car** is on the go.
Hi-ho, and off we go,
The **car** is on the go!

Thank You, Workers!

Children show their appreciation for school workers with this special Labor Day card.

Facts to Share

Labor Day salutes the contributions workers have made to the strength, prosperity, and well-being of our country. This holiday was first celebrated in New York City and is now observed annually on the first Monday in September.

Introducing the Activity

Explain that Labor Day is a holiday to honor America's workers. Have children brainstorm a list of different kinds of workers and talk about what they do. Help them understand that everything they need or want—from clothing to toys—as well as services such as mail delivery, transportation, and traffic control are provided by workers. Then ask children to name some of the workers and volunteers at your school. After discussing the work that these people do, invite each child to make a personalized thank you card to present to a worker at your school.

What to Do

1. Cut out the card along the bold lines (do not cut along the dashed line).

2. Choose a worker at your school to make the card for. Write that worker's name on the line at the top of the card. Write your name on the line at the bottom.

3. Fold the card in half along the dashed line.

4. Coat your hand with tempera paint and then make a handprint on the cover of the card. Set the card aside to dry.

Extension Activity

Invite your class to make an appreciation banner for the workers and volunteers in your school. First, take photos of school workers and volunteers. Then write "Celebrate Labor Day—Give Our Hard Workers a Hand!" on the center of a length of white bulletin board paper. Invite children to make colorful paint handprints around the edges of the banner. After the paint dries, have them sign their handprints and write or dictate a brief message for your school workers and volunteers. Display the banner in a prominent place in the school for all to enjoy.

MATERIALS

For each child:
- card pattern (page 114)
- scissors
- pencil

To share:
- tempera paint in several bright colors
- wide paintbrushes (one for each color of paint)

BOOK 📖 BREAK

Labor Day by Carmen Bredeson (Children's Press, 2000). Vibrant photos and simple text introduce young readers to this national holiday.

Columbus Sets Sail

Children create a booklet about the 1492
voyage of Christopher Columbus.

Facts to Share

In 1492, Christopher Columbus sailed with three ships—the *Nina*, *Pinta*,
and *Santa Maria*—hoping to find a shorter route to the Indies. His crew
spotted land on October 12, but they did not reach the Indies. Columbus
had landed on what we now know as North America! To remember this
historical voyage, our country observes Columbus Day in October each year.

Introducing the Activity

Share one of both books from "Book Break," or a book of your choice
about Christopher Columbus. Discuss Columbus's voyage and some of the
hardships he encountered (unknown territory, traveling day and night, bad
weather). Then invite children to make booklets about Columbus's trip.

What to Do

1. Cut out the booklet patterns. Color the cover and write your name on
   the line.

2. Glue flap 2a and flap 3a on the booklet pages where indicated.

3. Color the ships on page 1 and add sails. Color the ocean.

4. Fold the flap on page 2 to the right. Draw a sun on the left side of the
   page. Color the water at the bottom of the page and on the flap.

5. Fold the flap on page 2 to the left. Draw a moon on the right side of
   the page. Then draw a wavy line across the bottom of the flap to
   extend the ocean. Color the ocean blue and the sky black.

6. Fold the flap on page 3 to the right. Draw a sun and wispy clouds across
   the top of the page and flap to represent good weather.

7. Fold the flap to the left side of page 3. Color the cloud gray. Draw
   another gray cloud on the flap and add rain falling from the clouds.
   Draw a wavy line across the bottom of the flap to extend the ocean.
   Color the ocean.

8. On page 4, draw a land scene inside the circle (representing a telescope
   site). Color the rest of the page.

9. Sequence and stack the cover and pages. Then staple them together
   along the left side.

MATERIALS

For each child:
- booklet patterns
  (pages 115–117)
- scissors
- crayons
- glue stick

To share:
- stapler

BOOK 📖 BREAK

Columbus Day by Christina Mia Gardeski (Children's Press, 2000).
Highlights Columbus's explorations, discoveries, and related
holiday celebrations.

Follow the Dream: The Story of Christopher Columbus by Peter Sis
(Knopf, 2003). Christopher Columbus overcomes many obstacles to
fulfill his dream of travel.

Celebrate Veterans Day!

Children make this special booklet to share with others on Veterans Day.

Facts to Share

Veterans Day is celebrated on the eleventh day of the eleventh month of the year. At 11:00 in the morning, many Americans observe a moment of silence, remembering those who have served our country in the military.

Introducing the Activity

Provide children with background information on Veteran's Day by sharing a book from "Book Break." Afterward, tell children that *veterans* are the men and women who have served in the different branches of our country's military—the army, navy, air force, marines, and coast guard. Discuss why our country observes a special day for American veterans. Then have children make these booklets to emphasize the unique date of Veterans Day.

What to Do

1. Cut out the booklet cover and pages. Sequence and stack the pages behind the cover. Then staple the pages to the white construction paper, as shown, stapling along the top edge.

2. Write your name on the line at the bottom of the cover.

3. Use a pencil to trace the word on each page.

4. Decorate the construction-paper backing with glitter crayons and star stickers.

Extension Activity

Invite children to make banners to carry in a class Veterans Day parade! First, distribute 4½- by 6-inch sheets of white paper. Help children write "Thank You, Veterans!" on their paper and glue it to the center of a 9- by 12-inch sheet of red or blue construction paper. Next, have them use white crayon to decorate the colored paper with stars and stripes and then glue white crepe paper streamers to the bottom edge of their banners. Finally, teach them the song "On Veterans Day." Ask children to wear red, white, and blue to school on the day of the parade. Have them sing the song as they march and wave their banners.

BOOK 📖 BREAK

Veterans Day by Jacqueline S. Cotton (Children's Press, 2002). This book presents a history of Veterans Day and ways to honor our veterans.

Veterans Day by Robin Nelson (Lerner Publications, 2006). Simple text and photos help readers understand why we celebrate Veterans Day.

MATERIALS

For each child:
- booklet patterns (page 118)
- 4- by 8-inch piece of white construction paper
- scissors
- pencil
- glitter crayons
- star stickers (optional)

To share:
- stapler

On Veterans Day

(to the tune of "Yankee Doodle")

On Veterans Day, salute the flag.
Today's a special day.
Thank all the troops who served so true.
They served the U.S.A.!

Thank the troops who served so true,
On this special day.
They worked hard to keep us safe.
They served the U.S.A.!

Thanksgiving Turkey

Children make this paper-bag turkey to hold their thankful thoughts.

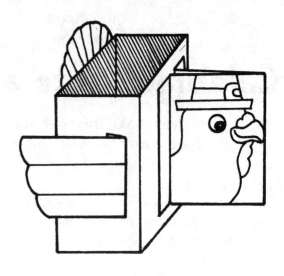

Facts to Share

Pilgrims most likely served wild duck, geese, and turkey at the harvest feast they shared with the Wampanoags in 1621. For many years, Thanksgiving was not celebrated regularly. In 1941, Congress made Thanksgiving an official holiday to be observed annually on the fourth Thursday in November. Today, Thanksgiving is a time for fun, family gatherings, and feasting—often with turkey as the featured dish!

Introducing the Activity

Invite children to tell about how they celebrate Thanksgiving. If desired, read *Thanksgiving* by Trudi Strain Trueit (see "Book Break" below) as a discussion starter. Then encourage children to share some things they are thankful for. Afterward, have them make these paper-bag turkeys filled with thankful thoughts. Children can use their turkeys as Thanksgiving table centerpieces and share their thankful thoughts with family members.

What to Do

1. Color and cut out the turkey patterns.

2. Glue a wiggle eye on each side of the head. Fold the head in half. Then fold the tab on each side toward the head. Glue the tabs to the front of the bag to attach the head to the bag "body."

3. Fold back the tab on each wing. Attach a wing to each side of the turkey body by gluing its tab to the bag.

4. Glue the tail to the top back edge of the body.

5. Read each sentence strip and write (or dictate) an ending to the sentence. Place the strips in your paper-bag turkey.

Extension Activity

Ask children to draw their favorite Thanksgiving foods on construction paper. Then have them cut out their pictures, glue them to disposable paper platters, and write the names of their food on the rim of the platters. Copy the poem "The Thanksgiving Feast" onto chart paper and display it on a bulletin board. Add children's completed platters around the poem. Recite the poem with children several times. Then invite children to take turns pointing out their platters and telling about their favorite foods.

> ∙∙∙∙∙∙∙∙ **BOOK 📖 BREAK** ∙∙∙∙∙∙∙∙
>
> *Thank You, Sarah: The Woman Who Saved Thanksgiving* by Laurie Halse Anderson (Aladdin, 2005). A determined woman campaigns for a national day of thanksgiving.
>
> *Thanksgiving* by Trudi Strain Trueit (Children's Press, 2006). Photos and text show how American families celebrate Thanksgiving.

∙∙∙∙∙ **MATERIALS** ∙∙∙∙∙

For each child:
- turkey patterns and sentence strips (pages 119–120)
- brown paper lunch bag, trimmed to 5 inches tall
- crayons
- scissors
- two wiggle eyes
- glue

The Thanksgiving Feast

Here's the Thanksgiving table.
Our feast is all laid out.
Here's the food that we like to eat.
It's all delicious, without a doubt!

We are thankful to have it.
We are lucky to share
All the wonderful dishes
That wait for us there!

Our Dream Team

Children create a class reminder of Dr. King's dream
for all people to live in harmony.

Facts to Share
Dr. Martin Luther King, Jr. was a famous African-American who taught
that all people could live together in peace. Although Dr. King's
birthday is on January 15th, the national holiday set aside to honor
this great man is observed on the third Monday in January.

Introducing the Activity
Tell children that every member of your class is important—as an
individual, a student, a friend, and a part of your class "team." Explain
that like Dr. King, your dream is that every member of your team will
show respect, friendship, and kindness to one another. Then help
children create this special bulletin board, titled "Our Dream Team,"
as a reminder that they belong to a team.

What to Do
1. Ask a classmate to use a pencil to trace around your arms and
   hands on the 12- by 18-inch sheet of white paper.

2. Use a crayon that matches your skin color to color the drawings of
   your arms and hands. Then cut out the shapes.

3. Draw a face on the paper plate to represent yourself. Color the
   face the color of your skin. For hair, glue on yarn or thin strips of
   construction paper.

4. Glue the 9-inch square of construction paper to the bottom of the
   paper-plate face to create a shirt. Write your name on the shirt.

5. Glue your arm cutouts to the sides of the shirt.

Extension Activity
Encourage children to write or dictate sentences on sentence strips
that tell how they might show kindness and friendship to each other.
Then copy the poem "Dr. King Dreamed" onto chart paper and post it
on a wall. Frame the poem with children's sentences. Finally, read the
poem several times, encouraging children to read along. Afterward,
invite them to read their sentences to the class.

• • • • • • • • BOOK 📖 BREAK • • • • • • • • •

Happy Birthday, Martin Luther King, Jr. by Jean Marzolo
(Scholastic, 2006). A simple story about Dr. King's life.

Martin Luther King, Jr. Day by Trudi Strain Trueit (Children's
Press, 2006). This book includes photographs and a variety of ways
to celebrate this unique holiday.

• • • • • MATERIALS • • • • •
For each child:
- 12- by 18-inch sheet of white
  construction paper
- pencil
- scissors
- white paper plate
- glue
- 9-inch square of red, white, or
  blue construction paper

To share:
- crayons, including flesh tones
- construction paper scraps
- yarn in various hair colors

Dr. King Dreamed

Dr. King dreamed
That he would see
A land of friendship
And equality.

A Special President

Children make and read this booklet with predictable text about our first president.

Who was

our

first

President?

George
Washington!

2

Facts to Share

Presidents' Day is a national holiday observed on the third Monday of February. Although the holiday was intended to honor George Washington on his birthday (which is February 22), many people also recognize Abraham Lincoln and other American presidents when commemorating this day. George Washington is the only president to have been elected by a unanimous vote.

Introducing the Activity

Ask children, "What is a President?" After sharing their ideas, lead children to conclude that the President of the U.S.A. is the leader of our country. Then display a picture of George Washington, inviting children to share any information they know about him. Write their responses on chart paper. Then correct any inaccurate information on the chart and add other interesting facts. You might also bring in and read a nonfiction picture book about George Washington. Afterward, invite children to make these booklets about this famous president.

What to Do

1. Cut out the booklet pages.

2. Sequence, stack, and staple the pages together at the top. Write your name on the back of the last page.

3. Color pages 2, 4, and 6.

4. Draw a picture of George Washington on page 8.

Extension Activity

Write "George Washington" on a sentence strip and place it in a pocket chart. Invite children to read the name with you as you track the name with your finger. Say it several more times, each time clapping each syllable in the name. Explain that each clap equals a *syllable*—a chunk or a part of a whole word. How many syllables are in "George Washington?" Repeat the activity using children's first and last names. How many syllables are in their names? Clap them out to find out!

MATERIALS

For each child:
- booklet pages (pages 121–122)
- scissors
- crayons

To share:
- stapler

• • • • • • • • • • • **BOOK 📖 BREAK** • • • • • • • • • • •

Presidents' Day by David F. Marx (Children's Press, 2002). This book introduces readers to two heroic American presidents.

Presidents' Day by Robin Nelson (Lerner Publications, 2002). This simple introduction to Presidents' Day features vibrant photographs and easy-to-read sentences.

Ready to Recycle!

Children create this booklet about recycling
to help raise environmental awareness.

Facts to Share ....

April 22nd marks the yearly observation of Earth Day, which was
established in 1970. As many as 20 million Americans took part in
activities on the very first Earth Day! Today people celebrate Earth
Day by planting trees, picking up litter, cleaning up parks, and
participating in other events that raise awareness of ecological issues.

Introducing the Activity ....

Invite children to tell about some ways in which they can help care for
our environment, such as planting trees, walking or riding bikes to
travel short distances, recycling, and reusing items such as plastic
shopping bags. After sharing, talk more specifically about how children
can help the environment by recycling. Discuss the kind of materials
they might recycle at home and school. Then have children make
these booklets to help reinforce the concept of recycling.

What to Do ....

1. Trace your hand on a sheet of construction paper that resembles
your skin tone. (Or ask a classmate to trace it for you.) Stack two
sheets of that flesh-tone paper behind the tracing and cut out
through all three layers. Repeat to make three more hand cutouts.

2. Glue each cutout to a separate sheet of green paper. On the last
green paper, glue only the left edge of the hand to the page to create
a flap.

3. Stack the pages, placing the page with the flap on the bottom.
Staple the pages together along the left side, leaving the flap free
to open and close.

4. Cut out the title, sentence, and can patterns. Glue the title to the
cover and write your name on the line.

5. Starting with the first page, glue a question to each page and a
square of the named material onto the hand. Glue the can cutout
on the page labeled "Whose hand recycles cans?"

6. Glue "My hand recycles!" to the last page. Lift the flap and glue
your photo under it.

MATERIALS

For each child:
- booklet patterns (page 123)
- six 6- by 9-inch sheets of
  construction paper in a variety
  of flesh tones
- pencil
- scissors
- six 9- by 12-inch sheets of
  green construction paper
- glue stick
- small square of newspaper,
  cardboard, and milk jug plastic
- small photo of self

BOOK 📖 BREAK

Earth Day by Robin Nelson (Lerner Publications, 2003). Presents
easy-to-read information about this special holiday.

Earth Day by Trudi Strain Trueit (Children's Press, 2006). Includes
photographs and a variety of ways to celebrate the holiday.

Memorial Poppies

Children craft this lift-the-petal poppy
necklace to observe Memorial Day.

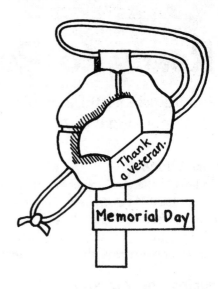

Facts to Share

Memorial Day began as a special day to decorate the graves of Civil
War soldiers with flowers. After World War I, red poppies became a
symbol of the holiday. In 1971, Congress made the last Monday in
May the official day to honor all those in the military who have lost
their lives in wars.

Introducing the Activity

To introduce children to Memorial Day, share one or both books listed
in "Book Break." Then explain that some veteran groups make and
sell pin-on "Buddy Poppies" in memory of those who lost their lives
fighting for our country. Afterward, invite children to make these
wearable poppies to observe Memorial Day.

What to Do

1. Cut out the poppy, necklace backing, and label.

2. Color the poppy center green and the petals dark red. Color the
necklace backing light red and the label light green.

3. Fold the necklace backing on the line. Glue the uncolored sides
together, leaving the area around the fold free of glue.

4. Cut along the lines between the poppy petals. Glue only the center
of the poppy to the necklace backing, leaving the petals free to fold
up and back.

5. If desired, glue green sequins to the center of the poppy. Then
glue the label to the green construction paper strip. Glue the strip
to the flower to create a stem.

6. Thread the yarn through the opening under the folded edge of the
necklace backing. Tie the ends together.

Extension Activity

To make poppy wreaths, ask children to write (or dictate) a sentence
about Memorial Day in the center of a white paper plate. Then have
them glue red die-cut flowers around the rim of their plates. They might
also add a green glitter-glue center to each flower. Display the wreaths
with the title "Memorial Day Thoughts."

● ● ● ● ● ● ● MATERIALS ● ● ● ● ● ● ●

For each child:

- poppy patterns (page 124)
- scissors
- green and red crayons
- glue
- green sequins (optional)
- 1- by 4-inch strip of green
  construction paper
- 28-inch length of green yarn

● ● ● ● ● BOOK 📖 BREAK ● ● ● ● ● ●

Let's Get Ready for Memorial Day by Lloyd Douglas (Children's
Press, 2003). A girl and her class visit a war memorial to learn
about Memorial Day.

Memorial Day by Christin Ditchfield (Children's Press, 2003.)
Simple text and photos introduce readers to Memorial Day.

American Flags All Around!

Children discover where they might see flags displayed with this Flag Day booklet.

I See a Flag

by _____ Joe

Facts to Share

On June 14, we observe Flag Day to commemorate the day our country adopted a national flag—June 14, 1777. On this day, American flags are flown over government buildings, as well as cemeteries, schools, and homes. Some cities and towns celebrate the day with parades and other special events.

Introducing the Activity

Use an American flag as a springboard for a discussion about Flag Day. Talk about the colors and symbols associated with the flag. Ask children to name places where they've seen the flag displayed. Then invite them to make these simple booklets to commemorate our national flag.

MATERIALS

For each child:
- booklet patterns (pages 125–127)
- scissors
- glue
- pencil
- crayons
- scissors

To share:
- stapler

What to Do

1. Cut out the booklet cover, pages, and flag patterns.

2. Sequence and stack the booklet pages behind the cover. Staple the booklet together along the left edge.

3. Glue a flag where indicated on the cover and each page.

4. Write your name on the line on the cover. Then fill in the blank on pages 1, 2, and 3 with *flag*. Write *flags* on the line on page 4.

5. Color the pictures on the cover and pages. Use red, white, and blue crayons to color the American flag each time it appears in the booklet.

Extension Activity

Hold up one small flag and ask children to tell what they see (a flag). Then hold up two or more flags. What do they see? (flags) Write *flag* and *flags* on chart paper. Explain that *flag* refers to one flag, while *flags* refers to more than one flag. Point out that an *s* is added to the word to make it plural. Then read a copy of the booklet. Each time children hear *flag*, have them give a single thumbs-up sign. When they hear *flags* have them hold up both thumbs.

BOOK 📖 BREAK

F Is For Flag by Wendy Cheyette Lewison (Grosset & Dunlap, 2002). Readers learn that our flag symbolizes unity and is a reminder that we all belong to one big family.

Flag Day by Kellie Bennett (Children's Press, 2003). Basic flag etiquette is included in this introduction to the festivities and traditions of Flag Day.

Hooray, Independence Day!

Children express their patriotic spirit with this star-spangled foldout booklet.

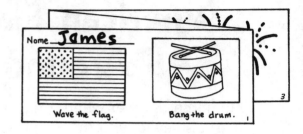

Facts to Share
On July 4, 1776, our country's leaders declared freedom from England—it was time for America to stand on its own! On this day each year, we observe Independence Day (also called America's birthday) to celebrate our freedom with family gatherings, picnics, parades, fireworks, and a variety of community events.

Introducing the Activity
Ask children to brainstorm a list of things they need to celebrate their birthdays. Then explain that Independence Day is also called America's birthday—and everyone is invited to the party! Invite volunteers to check off the things on the list that might also be used to celebrate Independence Day. Then have children think of other things—such as flags, parades, picnics, and fireworks—that are used in a July Fourth celebration. Afterward, invite children to make these foldout Independence Day booklets.

What to Do
1. Cut out the booklet pages and patterns.

2. Color the picnic basket, drum, and flag. Glue the flag and drum to the appropriate boxes on page 1.

3. On page 2, trace the word in the speech bubble. Add facial features to the child and color the picture. Glue the picnic basket to the box.

4. Use glitter crayons or glitter glue to draw fireworks on page 3.

5. Glue the booklet pages together where indicated. Accordion-fold the pages to create a foldout booklet.

Extension Activity
Hooray for red, white, and blue! Have children combine these all-American colors to make a patriotic snack. First, copy the recipe (at right) onto chart paper and place it in a center along with small plastic cups, plastic spoons, and containers of the needed ingredients—each with a plastic spoon for serving. Then invite children to read and follow the directions to make their snacks. (Check for food allergies ahead of time.)

• • • • • • • BOOK 📖 BREAK • • • • • • •

Independence Day by Robin Nelson (Lerner Publications, 2003). This book gives a brief overview why and how Independence Day is celebrated.

• • • • • MATERIALS • • • • •
For each child:
- booklet patterns (pages 128-129)
- crayons
- scissors
- glue
- pencil
- glitter glue (or glitter crayons)

All-American Snack
blueberries
whipped topping
red, white, and blue sprinkles
maraschino cherry

1. Spoon a layer of blueberries into a cup.
2. Cover the berries with whipped topping.
3. Add sprinkles.
4. Add the cherry.
5. Enjoy!

Voyage to America

Children recall facts about the voyage of the *Mayflower* with this lift-the-flap project.

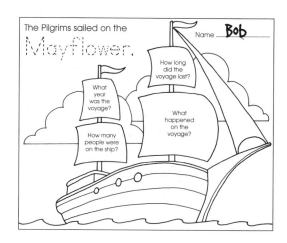

Facts to Share

The Pilgrims originally set sail for America aboard the *Speedwell*. This first ship was not seaworthy, though, so they returned to England and joined another group of settlers headed to America on the *Mayflower*. On September 6, 1620, The *Mayflower* left England carrying 102 passengers. After a long and stormy voyage, the ship finally reached Plymouth, Massachusetts on November 9.

Introducing the Activity

Read *The Mayflower* by Susan Whitehurst (see "Book Break") to provide children with information about the Pilgrims' voyage and experiences during the trip. After discussing the book, invite children to create these projects designed to reinforce facts about the ship. Encourage children to share their completed projects with partners by reading the question on each sail and then lifting the flaps to read the answers.

What to Do

1. Color and cut out the picture of the ship and the sail patterns.

2. Trace the name of the ship. Write your name on the line.

3. Glue the top part of each sail over its matching space on the ship, creating a flap with the sail.

4. Read the question on the large sail. Lift the sail and write (or dictate) a short sentence to answer the question.

Extension Activity

Once the Pilgrims reached Plymouth, they had a difficult struggle building their community. The first Thanksgiving was a celebration of surviving many hardships. Read and discuss *Sarah Morton's Day: A Day in the Life of a Pilgrim Girl* by Kate Waters (see "Book Break"). Then teach children "The Pilgrim Song." You might copy the song onto chart paper and have children track the words as they sing.

● ● ● ● ● ● BOOK 📖 BREAK ● ● ● ● ● ● ● ● ●

The Mayflower by Susan Whitehurst (PowerKids Press, 2002). This picture book presents the Pilgrim's dangerous ocean crossing aboard the *Mayflower*.

Sarah Morton's Day: A Day in the Life of a Pilgrim Girl by Scholastic Inc. (Scholastic Paperbacks, 1993). Photographs taken at Plimoth Plantation highlight this book about the life of a Pilgrim girl.

● ● ● ● ● MATERIALS ● ● ● ● ● ●
For each child:
■ ship and sail patterns
  (pages 130–131)
■ crayons
■ scissors
■ glue
■ pencil

The Pilgrim Song

(to the tune of "Over the River and Through the Woods")

Over the ocean, across the sea,
The Pilgrims sailed away.
The *Mayflower* ship took them on a trip
To Plymouth where they'd stay.

That's where the Pilgrims settled to live.
They worked hard every day.
The harvest was good so they had food
On that first Thanksgiving Day.

Picture Pouches

Children use this crafty pouch to share information about the Wampanoags.

Facts to Share

The Wampanoags lived in the Plymouth area long before the Pilgrims arrived in America. They built and operated both summer and winter settlements to make the best use of the weather, environment, and animal life characteristic of each season. The Wampanoags hunted wild game, fished and gathered clams, picked wild berries, and grew pumpkins, beans, and corn.

Introducing the Activity

Share facts about the Wampanoags of the early 1600s, using the books from "Book Break" as well as information you've gathered from your own research. Discuss the Wampanoags' way of life at that time—the foods they ate, their homes, and items used in their daily lives. Then have children create these pouches and picture cards of Wampanoag-related items to share with others.

What to Do

1. To make a pouch, stack the two sheets of light brown paper. Use scissors to round the bottom corners through both layers.

2. Glue the pouch shapes together along the sides and bottom, leaving the top open to create a pocket. Let the glue dry.

3. Write "The Wampanoags" on one side of the pouch. Draw a colorful design on the other side.

4. For the strap, punch a hole near the top of each side of the pouch. Tie each end of the yarn to a hole.

5. Draw a picture on each card to illustrate the word. Cut the cards apart and put them inside the pouch.

Extension Activity

The Wampanoags grew a trio of crops: tall, sturdy corn plants supported bean vines, and both plants shaded pumpkins that grew beneath them. Teach children the words and movements to "Corn, Beans, Squash." Then make a separate word card for *corn*, *beans*, and *squash*. As children sing the song, hold up the corresponding word when it appears in the lyrics.

BOOK 📖 BREAK

Tapenum's Day by Kate Waters (Scholastic Press, 1996). Photographs taken at Plimoth Plantation highlight the life of a Wampanoag boy.

The Wampanoags by Alice K. Flanagan (Children's Press, 1998). This book features the culture and history of the Wampanoags.

MATERIALS

For each child:
- picture cards (page 131)
- two 9- by 12-inch sheets of light brown construction paper
- scissors
- glue
- crayons
- 36-inch length of brown yarn

To share:
- hole punch

Corn, Beans, Squash

(to the tune of "Three Blind Mice")

Corn, beans, squash. Three good crops.
Hold up three fingers.

See how they grow. See how they grow.
Slowly raise hand to head level.

The corn grows straight up, so strong and tall.
Stand on tiptoe, arms at sides.

The beans twine 'round the corn so they don't fall.
Spin slowly in place.

The squash grows on the ground under them all.
Wave hands just above the floor.

Corn, beans, and squash.
Hold up three fingers.

Who Am I?

Children learn about early American heroes with this fun lift-the-flap book.

Facts to Share

There were many heroes in the early history of our country. For instance:

- George Washington led the first American army to fight for independence.
- Thomas Jefferson worked with four other great men to write the Declaration of Independence.
- Paul Revere made a courageous midnight ride to warn others that British troops were approaching.
- Betsy Ross is often credited with sewing the first American flag.
- On July 4, 1776, John Hancock, the first to sign the Declaration of Independence, wrote his name in large letters so that the King of England could "see it without his glasses."

Introducing the Activity

Display pictures of George Washington, Thomas Jefferson, Paul Revere, Betsy Ross, and John Hancock. Help children identify each person and talk briefly about his or her contribution to American history. Then invite children to make these lift-the-flap booklets to reinforce their knowledge of these famous early Americans.

What to Do

1. Cut out the cover, pages, and patterns.

2. Glue the title box on the cover where indicated. Write your name on the line.

3. Color the picture on each page. Then glue the flap for that page to the box where indicated.

4. Sequence and stack the pages behind the cover. Staple the booklet together at the top left corner.

MATERIALS

For each child:
- booklet patterns (pages 132–134)
- scissors
- glue
- crayons

To share:
- stapler

BOOK 📖 BREAK

Use these books to learn more about early American heroes.

George Washington (Rookie Biographies) by Wil Mara (Children's Press, 2003).

Betsy Ross (Rookie Biographies) by Wil Mara (Children's Press, 2006).

Thomas Jefferson (First Biographies) by Judy Emerson (Capstone Press, 2003).

Paul Revere (First Biographies) by Lisa Trumbauer (Capstone Press, 2004).

A Picture Book of John Hancock by David A. Adler (Holiday House, 2007).

Wagons Ho!

Children "pack" a lift-the-flap covered wagon for an imaginary cross-country move.

Facts to Share

Early pioneers packed all their belongings into covered wagons to move west. These families used their covered wagons as homes on the road as well as for moving vans to transport their entire households.

Introducing the Activity

Tape off a 4- by 12-foot area of floor space. Explain that this space was the size of a covered wagon in pioneer days. Everything needed for a move west was packed in that space—from clothing, furniture, and bedding to water and food. Show children pictures of the insides of covered wagons (check the books in "Book Break") and discuss the packing decisions that pioneers had to make when planning a move. Then have children decide what they would pack for a cross-country move when they make these lift-the-flap covered wagons.

What to Do

1. Cut out the wagon top. Glue it to the wagon where indicated, gluing only the top edge in place to create a flap.

2. Color the wagon. Then lift the flap and draw a few items that you would pack for a trip to the west. Or cut out magazine pictures of the items and glue them in the wagon.

3. Write (or dictate) the name of each item in the wagon.

Extension Activity

Have children make miniature covered wagons. For each child, remove the side with the perforated flaps from a single-serving cereal box. To begin, children paint their boxes with thick brown paint mixed with a bit of white glue. After the paint dries, they tape 4- by 8-inch sheets of white paper over their boxes to make bowed wagon covers. Then they glue four plastic bottle-cap "wheels" onto their wagons. Finally, children write (or dictate) a few sentences about their covered wagons on index cards to display with their projects.

• • • • • • • • • • • • BOOK 📖 BREAK • • • • • • • • • • • •

Daily Life in a Covered Wagon by Paul Erickson (Puffin, 1997). Use the photos and paraphrased text to help bring travel in a covered wagon to life.

Wagon Train (All Aboard Reading) by S. A. Kramer (Grosset & Dunlap,1997). Join the Wagon Train to learn what life was like for early pioneers.

• • • • • • MATERIALS • • • • • •

For each child:
■ wagon and wagon top patterns (pages 135–136)
■ crayons
■ magazines
■ scissors
■ glue

I Came to America

Children learn why many immigrants of long ago moved from their home countries to America.

Facts to Share ....

In the last part of the 19th century and the early 20th century, people from all over the world boarded great steamships to move to America. Most of these immigrants entered the U.S. through Ellis Island in New York, but many also entered through other American ports. People came to America to make better lives for themselves in a country that protected individual rights and freedom.

Introducing the Activity ....

Share one or both books listed in "Book Break" to give children information about the history of American immigration. After reading, discuss some of the reasons that people left their home countries for new lives in America. Then have children make these booklets to share with their families and friends.

What to Do ....

1. Cut out the booklet backing and pages.

2. Stack pages 1 and 2 on top of page 3. Staple the pages to the backing along the left side.

3. Write your name on the line near the title. Color the ship.

4. Draw faces on the people on each page. Then color the people.

5. On page 3, complete the sentence in the speech balloon by writing (or dictating) a reason someone might come to America.

Extension Activity ....

Write *diversity* on the chalkboard. Read the word and tell children that this is another word for different. Explain that America is made up of people from many different countries, backgrounds, beliefs, experiences, and so on. In other words, each person is unique. To emphasize children's uniqueness, have them draw self-portraits and then write (or dictate) a few things that make them special. Display the pages around a large copy of the poem "America Means Diversity!" Read the poem aloud with children several times. Then invite children to take turns telling about what makes them special

▪ ▪ ▪ ▪ ▪ ▪ ▪ ▪ ▪ ▪ ▪ ▪ BOOK 📖 BREAK ▪ ▪ ▪ ▪ ▪ ▪ ▪ ▪ ▪ ▪ ▪

Coming to America by Betsy Maestro Fuchs (Scholastic Press, 1996). This book gives information about America's history of immigration.

Ellis Island by Patricia Ryon Quiri (Children's Press, 1998). Easy-to-read text and photographs present facts about Ellis Island.

▪ ▪ ▪ ▪ ▪ MATERIALS ▪ ▪ ▪ ▪ ▪

For each child:
▪ booklet patterns
  (pages 137–138)
▪ scissors
▪ crayons

To share:
▪ stapler

America Means Diversity!

All of us are different,
As you can clearly see.
That's because America
Means diversity!

Then and Now

Children sort objects used by Americans
long ago from items used today.

When Did People Use It?

Then	Now
wagon wheel, quill pen, corn-husk doll	plastic doll, rubber tire, ball-point pen
These things were used long ago.	These things are used now.

Facts to Share

Long ago people lived in communities without electricity or running
water and used horses and wagons for transportation. Often, they made
their own household items. Today most of our household products are
machine-made in large factories. Electricity, automobiles, computers,
and many other inventions have created major changes in the daily life
of most Americans.

Introducing the Activity

Share the books listed in "Book Break" to provide visuals of how people
lived long ago and how they live today. Pause as you read to allow
children time to compare pictures in the books as well as to compare
them to things they are familiar with in their own environment and
experiences. After discussing, challenge children to sort pictures of
items from long ago and today to complete these classification charts.

What to Do

1. Write your name on the line above the chart. Color and cut out
the picture cards.

2. Decide which cards show pictures of items that were used long ago
and which ones show items that are used now. Sort the cards into
two groups: "Then" and "Now."

3. Glue each group of pictures to the appropriate side of the chart.

4. If desired, draw pictures of other items on each side of the chart.

Extension Activity

Set up a hands-on classification center. To prepare, use blue painter's
tape to divide a large table into two sections. Label one sentence strip
"Then" and another "Now." Tape each label to a section of the table.
Then gather a variety of household items to represent items from the
past and the present (see list at right). Put the items in a large basket.
Invite pairs of children to sort and classify the items by placing them in
the appropriate sections on the table. Encourage children to identify
and discuss items from the "Then" section that could also be used today.

MATERIALS

For each child:
- chart and picture cards
  (page 139)
- crayons
- scissors
- glue

Items for "Then"
beeswax candle
small cast-iron skillet
tin mug
raffia-stuffed pillow
corn husk "doll"

Items for "Now"
flashlight
nonstick skillet
plastic tumbler
poly-filled pillow
plastic doll

BOOK 📖 BREAK

Home: Then and Now and *School: Then and Now* by Robin Nelson
(Lerner Publications, 2003). The photos in these books illustrate
how life in America has changed over the centuries.

Our Flag

Children learn and share facts about the
American flag with this foldout booklet.

Facts to Share

The first American flag had thirteen red and white stripes and thirteen
white stars on a field of blue. Today's flag sports the same number of
stripes—to represent the thirteen original colonies—and fifty stars,
representing the number of states in our country today. On the flag,
red symbolizes courage, white liberty, and blue justice.

Introducing the Activity

Display an American flag. Explain that its design and colors symbolize
different things about our country. Share what the stars, stripes, and
colors symbolize. Then invite children to make these informative,
star-spangled booklets about the flag.

What to Do

1. Cut out the cover, pages, and patterns. Color the flag and write
your name on the title pattern. Glue the flag and title to the cover
where indicated.

2. Trace the color words on page 1, using a matching crayon to trace
red and *blue* and a pencil to trace *white*. Color the box beside each
word the matching color.

3. On page 2, write *50* on the line. Connect the dots to reveal a star.

4. Write *13* on the line on page 3. Starting with red, color the stripes
on the flag in an alternating red and white pattern.

5. On page 4, draw a picture of yourself as a proud American. You
might be wearing patriotic colors or waving an American flag!

6. Glue the cover and pages together where indicated. Accordion-fold
the booklet so that the cover is on top.

Extension Activity

Copy "A Flag for Me and You" onto chart paper. Invite children to
create their own American flags using craft materials, such as glitter
crayons, star stickers, and white paint pens. Afterward, read the poem
to children. Then have them recite it with you, pointing out each
feature on their flags as it is mentioned in the poem.

> **BOOK 📖 BREAK**
>
> *The American Flag* by Debbie L. Yanuck (Capstone Press, 2000).
> A look at the design, uses, and symbolic importance of the
> American flag.
>
> *The American Flag* by Lloyd G. Douglas (Children's Press, 2003).
> An introduction to the American flag and how it represents
> our country.

MATERIALS

For each child:
- booklet patterns
  (pages 140–142)
- scissors
- pencil
- crayons
- glue

A Flag for Me and You

Thirteen stripes.
Fifty stars,
Spread on a square of blue.

Put them together.
What do you have?
A flag for me and you!

A Symbolic Bell

Children make this little Liberty Bell booklet
about a great big American symbol.

Facts to Share

The Liberty Bell is a historical symbol of freedom. The bell was housed
in Independence Hall and was rung on many occasions, including the
announcement of the signing of the Declaration of Independence in
1776. This famous bell is also known for its crack, which kept returning
even after repeated repairs.

Introducing the Activity

Share *The Liberty Bell* by Lloyd G. Douglas (see "Book Break"). Discuss
the book, as well as "Facts to Share" and other information about the
bell that you've discovered in your own reading and research.
Afterward, invite children to make these mini-booklets to read to family
and friends. To follow-up the activity, copy "The Liberty Bell Song"
onto chart paper and track the words as you sing the song with children.

What to Do

1. Color and cut out the booklet cover and pages.

2. Write your name on the line on the cover.

3. Sequence and stack the pages behind the cover. Staple the booklet
together along the top edge.

Extension Activity

Point out that in the song, the Liberty Bell went *ding, dong, ding* before
it cracked, and *clack, clack, clack* afterwards. Use a fun guessing game to
introduce children to other onomatopoeic words—words that imitate
the sounds that things make. To begin, ask them questions such as
"What sound does a bee make?" (*buzz*) "What sound does a cat make?"
(*meow, purr*) and "What sound does a snake make?" (*hiss*) Then reverse
the activity to challenge children to name things that make a particular
sound (for instance, "What *growls?*").

> ● ● ● ● ● ● ● ● ● ● ● **BOOK 📖 BREAK** ● ● ● ● ● ● ● ● ● ● ●
>
> *The Liberty Bell* by Lloyd G. Douglas (Children's Press, 2003).
> Readers learn about the history and heritage of the Liberty Bell.

MATERIALS

For each child:
■ booklet patterns (page 143)
■ crayons
■ scissors
■ pencil

To share:
■ stapler

The Liberty Bell Song

(to the tune of "The Wheels on the Bus")

The Liberty Bell went ding, dong, ding.
"Hear me ring!" Ding, dong, ding.
The Liberty Bell went ding, dong, ding.
Freedom's ring.

Then one day the bell went clack, clack, clack.
Got a crack! Clack, clack, clack.
Then one day the bell went clack, clack, clack.
It rang no more.

Now the Bell is a symbol of liberty.
We are free—you and me!
An American symbol for all to see—
The Bell of Liberty.

The National Bird

Children learn about a majestic American symbol with this eagle puppet.

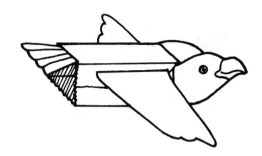

Facts to Share

Early leaders of our country chose the bald eagle as a symbol of American strength and freedom. The image of this regal bird can be found on U.S. currency, stamps, and is even on the Great Seal of the United States!

Introducing the Activity

Share *The Bald Eagle* by Lloyd G. Douglas (see "Book Break") and information from "Facts to Share." Then discuss the bald eagle as an American symbol. Afterward, invite children to create these bald eagle puppets to use as they sing "The Eagle Is a Special Bird."

What to Do

1. Cut out the heads and tail and the sentence patterns.

2. Color the eyes and beak yellow on both heads. Open the paper bag and glue a head to each side of the bottom of the bag, as shown. Glue the tips of the beaks together.

3. Glue the tail to the top open end of the bag, as shown.

4. Stack the two sheets of brown paper together and cut out long triangular wings through both layers. Glue a wing to each side of the paper-bag eagle.

5. Read each sentence pattern. Complete the sentence stem by writing (or dictating) something you know about the bald eagle. Glue two sentences to the underside of each wing.

Extension Activity

Help children learn more about the bald eagle's life in the wild. Title a large KWL chart "The Bald Eagle." Invite children to share what they already know about this bird. Write their ideas on the chart. Then write some things children would like to learn. Afterward, read and discuss *Bald Eagle* by Gordon Morrison (see "Book Break"). Complete the chart by adding new or correct information that children learned about the bald eagle.

MATERIALS

For each child:
- bald eagle and sentence patterns (page 144)
- brown paper lunch bag
- two 9- by 12-inch sheets of brown construction paper
- yellow crayon
- pencil
- scissors
- glue

The Eagle Is a Special Bird

(to the tune of "Yankee Doodle")

The eagle is a special bird.
It's powerful and free.
It represents America.
It stands for you and me!

This bald eagle's soaring high,
flying high and free.
It stands for America.
It stands for you and me!

BOOK 📖 BREAK

Bald Eagle by Gordon Morrison (Houghton Mifflin, 2003). The life cycle of the bald eagle is presented with interesting text and watercolor illustrations.

The Bald Eagle by Lloyd G. Douglas (Children's Press, 2003). This book tells how and why the bald eagle was chosen as a symbol for the United States.

Who Stands Tall?

Children learn about the Statue of Liberty
with this booklet about the famous statue.

Who Stands Tall?
by _Terry_

Facts to Share ....

The Statue of Liberty, a gift from the French, stands proudly in New
York Harbor as a symbol of friendship and freedom. The torch
represents enlightenment and the tablet is inscribed with the date our
country declared independence, July 4, 1776. The statue is made of
copper, which has weathered and turned green over the years.

Introducing the Activity ....

Share *The Statue of Liberty* by Lloyd G. Douglas (see "Book Break") as
well as other facts that you've discovered in your reading and research
about the statue. Display a picture of the statue, pointing out the torch,
crown, tablet, and gown. Then invite children to make these booklets
about this famous statue.

What to Do ....

1. Cut out the title, the four picture patterns, and booklet page 5.
Write your name on the cover pattern. Then glue each pattern to
a separate green sheet of paper.

2. Cut out the sentence boxes. Match and glue each one to the
booklet page with the corresponding picture.

3. Color all the pictures light green.

4. Sequence and stack the pages behind the cover. Then staple them
together along the left edge.

Extension Activity ....

Color and cut out enlarged copies of the torch, crown, tablet, gown,
and Statue of Liberty pictures on pages 145–146 (cut off the text under
the picture of the statue). Then copy each line of "Who Stands So
Tall?" on a separate sentence strip. Place the sentences and pictures in
a pocket chart. After reading the poem to children several times, have
them take turns sequencing the sentence strips and matching each
picture to the corresponding sentence.

.... BOOK 📖 BREAK ....

The Statue of Liberty by Lloyd G. Douglas (Children's Press, 2003).
Easy-to-read text introduces readers to America's national statue.

MATERIALS

For each child:
- booklet patterns
  (pages 145–146)
- six half-sheets of green
  construction paper
- scissors
- pencil
- glue
- green crayon

To share:
- stapler

Who Stands So Tall?

Here is her torch.
Here is her crown.
Here is her tablet,
And here is her gown.
Can you guess who stands so tall?
The Statue of Liberty—freedom for all!

Our Patriotic Uncle

Children make this puppet to learn about Uncle Sam and what he symbolizes.

Facts to Share

Uncle Sam's origins began with Sam Wilson, a hard-working, honest man who supplied meat to the U.S. Army. Soldiers began to interpret the initials U.S. on the meat crates as *Uncle Sam*, in reference to Sam Wilson. Over the years, the concept and images of Uncle Sam have evolved this character into a patriotic symbol of our country.

Introducing the Activity

Write *Uncle Sam* on chart paper and display one or more pictures of the character. Tell children that all Americans share an uncle—Uncle Sam! Point out and then trace the beginning initials of his name. Explain Uncle Sam's initials are *U. S.*, the same initials used for *United States*. Then call attention to the patriotic colors and symbols on his clothing. Ask children to name another American symbol that sports these same colors and symbols (the flag). Afterward, have children make these Uncle Sam puppets. Copy the poem "Uncle Sam—That's Me!" onto chart paper and invite children to use their puppets while reciting the poem.

What to Do

1. Color the Uncle Sam patterns red, white, and blue. Then cut out all the patterns.

2. Use a paper brad to connect each arm and leg to the body.

3. Stretch and shape the cotton ball into a beard (or goatee). Glue it to Uncle Sam's chin.

4. Glue the craft stick to the back of the body.

Extension Activity

Uncle Sam isn't the only one with initials—everyone has them! Explain that initials are the first letters in a person's first and last name. Then have children write their own initials in large lettering and decorate them in patriotic colors. They might use craft materials such as glitter glue, construction paper scraps, craft foam, yarn, and stamp pads. Display the initials near a list of children's names. Then have children match each set of initials with the correct name.

● ● ● ● ● ● ● ● ● ● ● ● ● **BOOK 📖 BREAK** ● ● ● ● ● ● ● ● ● ● ● ●

Uncle Sam (First Facts) by Debbie L. Yanuck (Capstone Press, 2003). Follows the evolution of Uncle Sam from political cartoon to American symbol.

● ● ● ● ● **MATERIALS** ● ● ● ● ●

For each child:
- Uncle Sam patterns (page 147)
- crayons
- scissors
- 4 paper brads
- glue
- cotton ball
- jumbo craft stick

I'm Uncle Sam— That's Me!

Can you guess just who I am?
I parade on Independence Day.
With stars on my hat and stripes on my pants,
I stand for the U.S.A.!

I'm always dressed in red, white, and blue.
I have a white goatee.
Can you guess just who I am?
I'm Uncle Sam—that's me!

The President's Home

Children learn about the White House and its most important resident with this lift-the-flap project.

Facts to Share

George Washington helped choose a site and plans for a home and office to be built for the U.S. President. John Adams was the first President to live in the President's House. Over the years, this famous home became known as the White House. It is located at 1600 Pennsylvania Avenue in Washington, D.C.

Introducing the Activity

Display the cover of *The White House* by Lloyd G. Douglas (see "Book Break"). Ask children to name the house and tell who lives there. Then read the book to the class. Afterward, discuss what children learned about the White House. Finally, invite them to make these lift-the-flap White House projects to share with others.

What to Do

1. Cut out the patterns. Glue the two sides of the White House together where indicated. Then staple the left and right flaps to the corresponding sides of the building (match the dots and stars). Glue the flag to the right side of the roof.

2. Lift the flap on the left and draw a picture of the current president in the box. Write the President's name on the line.

3. Lift the flap on the right side and write (or dictate) an ending to the sentence.

4. Close both flaps and color the White House and flag.

Extension Activity

Dig deeper into what the president does by sharing *If I Were President* by Catherine Stier (see "Book Break"). Discuss with children what they might do each day if they were President of the United States. What would they like best about being President? Have them write (or dictate) their responses on white construction paper and illustrate their pages. Invite children to share their completed pages with the class.

MATERIALS

For each child:
■ White House patterns (pages 148–149)
■ scissors
■ glue stick
■ crayons

To share:
■ stapler

BOOK 📖 BREAK

If I Were President by Catherine Stier (Albert Whitman & Company, 1999). This easy picture book explains the different duties of the president.

The White House by Lloyd G. Douglas (Children's Press, 2003). Simple text and pictures introduce children to the White House.

Johnny's Apple Seed

Children celebrate Johnny Appleseed's birthday with this "a-peeling" booklet about apple trees.

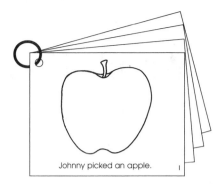

Johnny picked an apple.

Facts to Share

John Chapman, also known as Johnny Appleseed, planted and sold apple trees throughout the Midwest. He made friends with the Native Americans and new settlers in the region, and many towns were established near his apple groves.

Introducing the Activity

Display pictures of Johnny Appleseed. (You might use pictures from the books listed in "Book Break.") Then share facts about this legendary man. After discussing, invite children to make these easy-to-read booklets about the life cycle of apple trees.

What to Do

1. Cut out the booklet pages. Complete each page as described.
   page 1: Color the apple.
   page 2: Use the black stamp pad to make "fingerprint" seeds on the apple core.
   page 3: Color the hand. Glue an apple seed onto the hand (or make a fingerprint seed).
   page 4: Color the ground brown. Add glitter-glue raindrops in the sky.
   page 5: Color the tree.
   page 6: Color the branch. Then draw green leaves on it.
   page 7: Color the branch and leaves. Paint some pink flowers.
   page 8: Color the tree. Then add red sticker dot "apples."

2. Punch a hole in the top left corner of each page where indicated.

3. Sequence the pages and bind them with the binder ring. Then read the story again and again!

Extension Activity

Cut out a large tree shape from green bulletin board paper. Copy the song "It's Johnny Appleseed" onto the tree to display. Then sing the song, tracking the words as children sing along. Later, help them identify the rhyming word pairs in the song and brainstorm other words that rhyme with each pair.

BOOK 📖 BREAK

Johnny Appleseed by Christin Ditchfield (Children's Press, 2003). A mix of full-color and black-and-white photographs introduce readers to Johnny Appleseed.

Johnny Appleseed by Gwenyth Swain (First Avenue Editions, 2001). This book focuses on facts about Johnny Appleseed.

MATERIALS

For each child:
- booklet pages (pages 150–151)
- scissors
- crayons
- one apple seed
- small red sticker dots
- binder ring

To share:
- black stamp pad
- white glue (optional)
- pink tempera paint
- paintbrushes
- hole punch

It's Johnny Appleseed!

(to the tune of "She'll Be Coming Round the Mountain")

Oh, John Chapman planted lots of apple seeds.
And those tiny seeds grew into apple trees.
Around the towns and on the ranches,
They grew leaves and many branches.
Lots of apples grew on all those apple trees.

Do you know John Chapman has another name?
Do you know John Chapman has another name?
Yes, it's Johnny Appleseed—
That's his nickname, yes indeed!
Johnny Appleseed and John Chapman are
   the same!

Which President?

Children unfold interesting facts about our
16th president with this tall booklet.

Facts to Share

Abraham Lincoln, the 16th president of the U.S., loved to read when
he was young. He walked miles and miles to borrow books and return
them to his neighbors. Although he attended school for only a year,
Lincoln spent his entire life learning as much as possible. Not only was
he big on learning, Lincoln was a big man. He measured six feet, four
inches tall. When wearing his 11-inch tall stovepipe hat, where he kept
important papers, Lincoln stood a whopping 7 feet 3 inches!

Introducing the Activity

Display a few pictures of Abraham Lincoln. (You might use pictures
from the books in "Book Break.") Encourage children to tell what they
know about Lincoln. Then share facts and other interesting information
about this famous man. After discussing, invite children to make these
easy-to-read booklets of Lincoln facts.

What to Do

1. Cut out the booklet pages. Glue the pages together where indicated.

2. Write your name on the line at the bottom.

3. Color the entire picture.

4. Accordion-fold the pages, keeping the title page on top.

Extension Activity

To give children practice in comparing heights, cut out several black
construction paper hats, each a different height. Then label a set of
index cards with *tall*, *taller*, and *tallest*. Place the hats and cards in a
pocket chart. Encourage children to choose three hats, sequence them
by height, and then match the corresponding word card to each hat.

BOOK 📖 BREAK

Abe Lincoln: The Boy Who Loved Books by Kay Winters (Aladdin,
2006). Introduces Abraham Lincoln and his love of books
and reading.

Abraham Lincoln: A Life of Respect by Sheila Rivera (Lerner
Publishing Group, 2006). This book explores the life, accomplishments, and influence of Abraham Lincoln.

Let's Read About . . . Abraham Lincoln by Sonja Black (Scholastic,
2002). Readers learn why Abraham Lincoln is thought to be one
of America's greatest presidents.

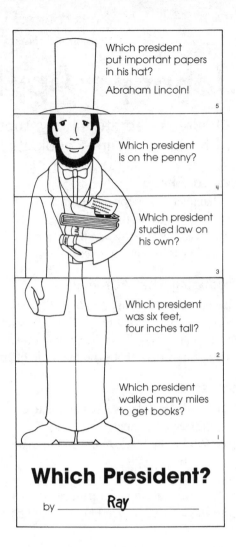

Which President?

by _____ Ray _____

MATERIALS

For each child:
- booklet patterns
  (pages 152–153)
- scissors
- glue stick
- crayons

The Plant Doctor

Children learn interesting facts about George Washington Carver with this booklet.

Facts to Share

As a child, the frail young George Washington Carver spent a lot of time exploring nature and learning about plants. As his plant knowledge grew, he became known as the Plant Doctor. Years later, Mr. Carver worked as a teacher and scientist at Tuskegee Institute in Alabama, where he invented many different uses for peanuts and other plants.

Introducing the Activity

Share one or more books from "Book Break" to introduce children to George Washington Carver. Then discuss the many ways this African-American inventor helped farmers and others with his work. Afterward, have children create these peanut-shaped booklets to reinforce their knowledge of Mr. Carver.

What to Do

1. Cut out the booklet backing, cover, and pages.

2. If desired, place the cover on top of the plastic canvas. Then lightly rub the cover with a brown crayon to create a peanut-like texture. Or just color the cover brown. Write your name on the line.

3. Sequence, stack, and staple the pages to the booklet backing along the top edge. Then color the pictures on pages 1–3.

4. On page 4, draw some things that are made with peanuts, such as a jar of peanut butter, candy bar, and bottle of peanut oil. Then color George Washington Carver (on the right).

Extension Activity

Tell children that George Washington Carver invented many things using peanuts and sweet potatoes. Write *peanut* and *potato* on chart paper, say the words, and have children identify their beginning sounds. Then ask children to brainstorm other words that begin with *p*. Finally, have them write and illustrate other *p* words on paper peanut shapes to display on a word wall.

MATERIALS

For each child:
▪ booklet patterns (pages 154–156)
▪ scissors
▪ crayons

To share:
▪ plastic canvas (optional)
▪ stapler

BOOK 📖 BREAK

George Washington Carver by Lynea Bowdish (Children's Press, 2004). An introduction to George Washington Carver, his work, and his inventions.

George Washington Carver: A Life of Devotion by Robin Nelson (Lerner Publications, April 2007). This book tells about George Washington Carver and his devotion to teaching, nature, and helping farmers.

A Sensible Learner

Children create a class book about Helen Keller
and her amazing accomplishments.

Helen Keller learned to talk.

Facts to Share ....

As a young child, Helen Keller lost her ability to see, hear, and speak.
At age six, her teacher, Anne Sullivan, taught Helen how to use finger
spellings to communicate with others. Later, Helen learned how to read
and write in Braille. She also learned how to speak and lip-read by
touching a speaker's lips. After graduating from college, Helen became
a lecturer and advocate for the deaf and blind.

Introducing the Activity ....

Read aloud *Helen Keller* by Pamela Walker (see "Book Break"). Have
children cover their eyes as you read a page containing pictures. Ask
them to cover their ears while you read another page. Then challenge
them to answer a question about the text—without speaking! After
conducting this sense-blocking experiment, invite children to use
all their senses as you read the entire book. Afterward, discuss the
difficulties Helen Keller faced when trying to communicate and learn
without the ability to hear, see, or speak. Then, on a sheet of white
paper, write "Helen Keller learned to ___." Copy a class supply of the
page. Invite children to complete the pages to use in a class book about
Helen Keller.

What to Do ....

1. Draw a picture of something that Helen Keller learned to do.

2. Write (or dictate) a completion to the sentence to describe
your picture.

To make the class booklet:

1. Stack the completed pages between the two sheets of construction
paper covers and staple along the left edge. Use the marker to write
"What Helen Keller Learned" on the cover.

Extension Activity ....

Copy "Helen Keller Had Courage" onto chart paper. Teach children the
song, tracking the words as they sing each line. Each time you repeat the
song, have children replace *learn* with *change, speak, read, teach,* or *help.*

MATERIALS

For each child:
- copy of programmed paper (prepared in "Introducing the Activity")
- crayons
- pencil

For the class:
- stapler
- two 9- by 12-inch sheets of construction paper (in a light color)
- marker

Helen Keller Had Courage

(to the tune of "For He's a Jolly Good Fellow")

Oh, Helen Keller had courage.
Oh, Helen Keller had courage.
Oh, Helen Keller had courage,
'Though she could not see or hear.

With courage she could **learn**.
With courage she could **learn**.
Oh, Helen Keller had courage
'Though she could not see or hear.

BOOK 📖 BREAK

Helen Keller by Pamela Walker (Children's Press, 2001). This
biography introduces the inspirational Helen Keller.

A Picture Book of Helen Keller by David A. Adler (Holiday House,
1991). This simple picture book presents Helen's childhood
accomplishments and early college years.

A Courageous Woman

Children create posters to describe the personality and actions of Rosa Parks.

Rosa Parks was

determined

by Janna

Facts to Share

In 1955, an African-American woman named Rosa Parks was arrested for refusing to give up her seat on a bus to a white passenger. Her actions launched the Montgomery Bus Boycott, which lasted 381 days. Mrs. Parks was a leader in the Civil Rights Movement and worked hard to help end racism and segregation. In 1999, she was awarded the Congressional Gold Medal of Honor, the highest and most distinguished award a citizen can receive from our government.

Introducing the Activity

After sharing and discussing a book about Rosa Parks (see "Book Break"), invite children to brainstorm words that describe her and her actions, such as *courageous, fair, determined, caring,* and *hard-working.* List their responses on chart paper. Then have children create these posters, using words from the list to describe Rosa Parks.

What to Do

1. Choose a word from the list that describes Rosa Parks. Write the word on the line to complete the sentence on the poster.

2. Draw a picture in the box to represent the sentence.

3. Write your name on the line at the bottom of the poster.

Extension Activity

Write the words from the list in "Introducing the Activity" on index cards. Read each word card to children, helping them sound out the syllables. Then challenge children to group the words by syllable count. Have them display each group of words in a pocket chart. Finally, sing "Do You Know of Rosa Parks?" with children. Before repeating the song, ask a volunteer to choose a word from the pocket chart that has a specific syllable count, such as a two-syllable word. Then sing the song again, replacing *courageous* with the word selected by the child.

• • • • • • • • • • BOOK 📖 BREAK • • • • • • • • • •

I Am Rosa Parks by Rosa Parks (Puffin, 1999). In this autobiography, Rosa Parks describes her experiences surrounding the Montgomery Bus Boycott.

Rosa Parks by Wil Mara (Children's Press, 2006). This book presents the life of Rosa Parks, civil rights pioneer.

• • • • • MATERIALS • • • • •

For each child:
■ poster pattern (page 157)
■ crayons
■ pencil

Do You Know of Rosa Parks?

(to the tune of "Do You Know the Muffin Man?")

Do you know of Rosa Parks,
Rosa Parks, Rosa Parks?
Do you know of Rosa Parks?
A very **courageous** woman!

Warrior for Farm Workers

Children make a booklet to learn about how Cesar Chavez helped improve life for farm workers.

Facts to Share

Cesar Chavez spent most of his adult life trying to improve the lives of migrant farm workers. He organized and led an organization called the United Farm Workers, which worked to improve working conditions, wages, housing, and education for farm workers. To help achieve his goals, Chavez led nonviolent protests, boycotts, and strikes. His lifelong motto was "It can be done."

Introducing the Activity

Share one or both books from "Book Break" to introduce children to Cesar Chavez. Discuss how he made life better for migrant farm workers. Then ask children to tell how the things he achieved in his life reflect his personal motto of "It can be done." Afterward, invite them to make these booklets that summarize the life work of Cesar Chavez.

What to Do

1. Cut out the booklet patterns. Write your name on the cover.

2. Sequence the pages behind the cover. Then staple the stack of pages to the top of the backing where indicated.

3. Draw a picture on pages 2, 3, and 4 to illustrate the text.

4. Color the picture on the left side of the booklet backing.

Extension Activity

Encourage children to brainstorm basic things that American workers need to have good working conditions (such as a safe environment, good equipment, running water, electricity, access to medical care, and an opportunity to improve their skills or education). List their suggestions on chart paper. Then ask them to draw pictures that represent items on the list. Copy the poem "Cesar Chavez Cared" onto another sheet of chart paper and display this with children's pictures. After reading the poem several times with the class, invite children to tell about their pictures.

● ● ● ● ● ● ● BOOK 📖 BREAK ● ● ● ● ● ● ●

Cesar Chavez by Susan Eddy (Children's Press, 2003). A great book to introduce young children to this inspiring man.

Harvesting Hope by Kathleen Krull (Harcourt Children's Books, 2003). Beautiful art illustrates this story of Cesar Chavez's life.

● ● ● ● MATERIALS ● ● ● ●

For each child:
- booklet patterns (page 158)
- crayons
- scissors

To share:
- stapler

Cesar Chavez Cared

Cesar Chavez cared
    about farm workers and their needs.
He gave them his support
    in his words and in his deeds.
He worked to win them rights
    and to get them better pay.
He worked so that their lives
    would improve in every way.

One Man in Orbit

Youngsters learn about John Glenn and *Friendship 7*
with this lift-the-flap space capsule.

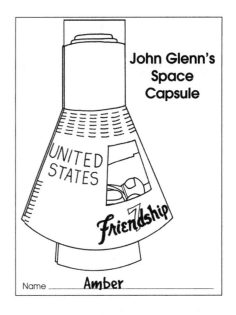

John Glenn's
Space
Capsule

Name _____ Amber

Facts to Share

In 1962, John Glenn was the first American astronaut to orbit the
earth, circling it three times in a space capsule called *Friendship 7*—
which was large enough to hold only one astronaut. Glenn had to
remain seated during the nearly five-hour flight. Unlike the spacecraft
landings of today, *Friendship 7* splashed down in the Atlantic Ocean and
John Glenn was transported to land by ship. Many years later he flew in
space again, this time on the space shuttle, to became America's oldest
astronaut at age 77.

Introducing the Activity

Use pictures and paraphrased text from the books listed in "Book
Break" (or other resources of your own choice) to share facts about
John Glenn. Explain that Glenn wore a bulky spacesuit and remained
strapped in his seat during his orbit in the small, cramped *Friendship 7*.
Then have children create these lift-the-flap space capsules to reinforce
their understanding of John Glenn's historic space flight.

What to Do

1. Color and cut out the patterns.

2. Cut out the window on the space capsule. Glue the clear rectangle
   to the back of the opening to create a window.

3. Glue the space capsule over the picture of the inside view, gluing
   only where indicated to create a flap.

MATERIALS

For each child:
- space capsule patterns (pages 159–160)
- crayons
- scissors
- 1- by 2-inch rectangle of clear transparency or page protector
- glue stick

Extension Activity

The *Friendship 7* was small compared to today's space shuttle. Display
pictures of both for children to discuss and compare. Encourage them to
use opposite pairs when making comparisons between the spacecrafts,
their equipment, and other characteristics of each kind of space travel.
For example, they might compare the size (*big/little*) and speed
(*slow/fast*) of the spacecrafts, the length of their flights (*short/long*),
the altitude they traveled (*low/high*), and the weight of the astronauts'
gear (*heavy/light*).

● ● ● ● ● ● ● BOOK 📖 BREAK ● ● ● ● ● ● ● ●

Godspeed, John Glenn by Richard Hilliard (Boyds Mills Press, 2006).
This informative biography chronicles John Glenn's historic flight
aboard *Friendship 7*.

John Glenn (American Lives) by Elizabeth Raum (Heinemann, 2005).
This introduction to John Glenn offers interesting information about
his life and historic flight, as well as the *Friendship 7*.

A Woman in Space

Children make this easy-to-read booklet about America's first female astronaut.

Facts to Share

Sally Ride, America's first female astronaut, flew into space twice on the space shuttle, *Challenger*. While in space, she was responsible for operating the shuttle's robot arm and conducting research and experiments. Sally Ride was one of five astronauts on the *Challenger*, which was large enough for the crew to move about and even exercise in!

Introducing the Activity

Display pictures of Sally Ride and the interior and exterior of the space shuttle. Share facts about this famous astronaut, encouraging children to tell what they know about Sally Ride and the space shuttle. Afterward, invite them to make these easy-to-read booklets about America's first female astronaut.

What to Do

1. Cut out the booklet pages and patterns. Glue each pattern to its corresponding page.

2. Write your name on the cover. Then color Earth (at top left) light blue and the sky light black. If desired, add a few star stickers to the sky.

3. Color pages 2–5. On page 5, trace Sally Ride's name with a pencil.

4. Sequence the pages and stack them behind the cover. Staple the booklet together at the top left corner.

Extension Activity

Write *Sally*, *space*, and *shuttle* on the chalkboard. Say each word and have children identify its beginning letter. Then have them brainstorm a list of other space-related words that begin with *s*, such as *sun*, *star*, *sky*, *solar system*, *satellite*, and *space station*. Write each word on an index card. Then, on a sentence strip, write "Sally sees a _____." Place the sentence strip in a pocket chart and have children take turns using the word cards to complete the sentence.

BOOK 📖 BREAK

Sally Ride: Astronaut, Scientist, Teacher by Pamela Hill Nettleton (Picture Window Books, 2003). This book tells about Sally Ride's experiences in space, including how she worked and ate meals on the space shuttle.

MATERIALS

For each child:
- booklet patterns (pages 161–163)
- scissors
- glue stick
- crayons
- small silver star stickers (optional)
- pencil

To share:
- stapler

Fiesta!

Children learn about Mexico's most celebrated holiday with this bilingual booklet.

Mexican Independence Day

Party Time!   **¡Fiesta!**

Facts to Share

On September 16, the people of Mexico gather to celebrate their country's independence from Spain. It was on this day in 1810 that Father Miguel Hildago rang the bell of his church to call Mexicans to fight for liberty. To commemorate this event, the ringing of the bell is re-enacted every year in plazas across Mexico. The holiday is also celebrated with flag-waving, parades, music, and dancing.

Introducing the Activity

Display pictures of a Mexican Independence Day celebration. (You might use pictures from the books listed in "Book Break.") Share facts about the history and traditions of this holiday. Then invite children to make these bilingual booklets about Mexican Independence Day. Before they begin, review both the English and Spanish words used in the booklet with children.

What to Do

1. Color and cut out the booklet backing and pages.

2. Sequence the pages that contain sentences in English. Stack them behind the cover labeled "Party Time!" and staple to the left side of the backing.

3. Sequence the pages containing Spanish words behind the cover labeled "Fiesta!" Staple to the right side of the backing.

Extension Activity

Reinforce children's word knowledge with bilingual puzzles. First, glue pictures of common items in the center of sentence strips. Write the English word for each item on one side of the picture and the Spanish word on the other side. Then puzzle-cut each sentence strip into three parts to create a separate piece for the picture and each word. Finally, have children assemble the puzzles and then read the English and Spanish words for each picture.

MATERIALS

For each child:
- booklet patterns (pages 164–166)
- crayons
- scissors

To share:
- stapler

BOOK 📖 BREAK

Look What Came From Mexico by Miles Harvey (Franklin Watts, 1999). Use the "Festivities and Holidays" section to discover how Mexican Independence Day is celebrated.

Mexican Independence Day and Cinco De Mayo by Dianne M. Macmillan (Enslow Publishers, 1997). Explores the history and traditions of two Mexican celebrations.

Mexico (A to Z) by Justine and Ron Fontes (Children's Press, 2004). Simple text and photos introduce the people, culture, and history of Mexico.

Celebrate the Harvest!

Children learn about harvest celebrations around the world with this shape booklet.

Facts to Share

During harvest celebrations around the world, people express appreciation for the fruit of the land. The following shows some harvest festivals for different countries and the crops that are associated with them:

• India: Rice Harvest Festival, rice
• Ghana and Nigeria: Yam Festival, yams
• Israel: Jewish Harvest Festival, fruit
• China: Mid-Autumn Festival, general harvest
• America: Thanksgiving, general harvest

Introducing the Activity

Share and discuss pictures of different foods being harvested. (You might use pictures from the books in "Book Break.") Explain that many countries hold festivals to celebrate their harvests. Talk about the kinds of foods that are harvested and where they might be grown (see "Facts to Share"), pointing out each location on a globe or world map. Then invite children to make these booklets about harvest celebrations.

What to Do

1. Cut out the booklet patterns. Complete each page as described.

cover: Write your name on the line.

page 1: Color the rice bag. Glue rice in and around the opening of the bag.

page 2: Place the page on top of the shelf-lining square. Lightly color the yams with a crayon to create a textured appearance.

page 3: Color the bowl. Draw your favorite fruits in the bowl.

backing and page 4: Color the cornucopia. Draw a few of your favorite foods that grow from plants in the opening of the cornucopia.

2. Sequence and stack the pages behind the cover. Then staple them to the right side of the backing where indicated.

MATERIALS

For each child:
■ booklet patterns (pages 167–169)
■ scissors
■ crayons
■ white glue

To share:
■ uncooked white rice
■ 5-inch squares of textured shelf lining
■ stapler

BOOK 📖 BREAK

Fall Harvest by Gail Saunders-Smith, Ph.D. (Capstone Press, 1998). Readers learn how different kinds of crops are harvested.

Harvest by Kris Waldherr (Walker & Company, 2001). A girl and her mother harvest fruits, vegetables, herbs, and flowers from their garden.

It's Sukkah Time! by Latifa Berry Kropf (Kar-Ben Publishing, 2003). Preschoolers celebrate Sukkot in this festive photo-illustrated book.

Fall

Ramadan Lantern

Children learn about Ramadan with this colorful lantern.

Name **Robert**

My lantern can
glow _____ in the night.

Facts to Share

Ramadan is a time to focus on faith and charity. For an entire month, people fast during the day, then eat small meals with family and friends after sunset. In Egypt, after the daylong fast, colorful lanterns light the streets and homes. Egyptian children enjoy swinging these festive *fanoos* and singing special songs.

Introducing the Activity

Use *Holidays Around the World: Celebrate Ramadan and Eid Al-Fitr* by Deborah Heiligman (see "Book Break") to share photos and information about Ramadan with children. Then have them brainstorm words that describe a lighted lantern, such as *beam, glow, shine,* and *twinkle.* Write children's responses on chart paper and review the list with them. Afterward, have them choose words from the list to use on these Ramadan lanterns.

What to Do

1. Cut out the lantern pattern. Use glitter crayons to color the base and dome of the lantern.

2. Brush the glue mix on one small section of the lantern globe at a time, covering the glue with colorful tissue paper scraps. Continue until the globe is covered with tissue paper. Let the glue dry.

3. Write (or dictate) a word from the list to complete the sentence.

Extension Activity

Stretch children's vocabulary by asking them to name other things that make or give off light (such as *lamp, flashlight, sun, nightlight, lightning bug,* and *star*). Write their responses on chart paper. Then invite children to choose words from the list to use in sentences.

▪ BOOK 📖 BREAK ▪

Holidays Around the World: Celebrate Ramadan and Eid Al-Fitr by Deborah Heiligman (National Geographic Children's Books, 2006). This photo-illustrated book covers the history of Ramadan as well as contemporary celebrations in various countries.

MATERIALS

For each child:
- lantern pattern (page 170)
- scissors
- glitter crayons
- white glue thinned with water
- paintbrush
- tissue paper scraps

A Little Lamp

Children learn about a Diwali tradition
when they create this holiday lamp.

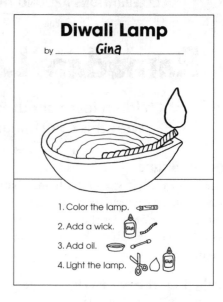

Diwali Lamp
by _____ Gina _____

1. Color the lamp.
2. Add a wick.
3. Add oil.
4. Light the lamp.

Facts to Share

Diwali, also called the Festival of Lights, is a Hindu celebration that
lasts five days and nights. The festival celebrates the victory of good
over evil. To prepare for Diwali, people in India clean their homes and
open their windows to welcome in prosperity. They also light clay
lamps and exchange gifts.

Introducing the Activity

Use the books listed in "Book Break" and other resources of your choice
to introduce children to Diwali. Tell them that Diwali is a joyous time
filled with lights, gifts, sweets, and fireworks. Then demonstrate how
to decorate the Diwali lamp pattern (see directions). Read aloud each
step on the pattern before completing it. Afterward, invite children to
read and follow the directions to make their own lamps.

What to Do

1. Write your name on the line.

2. Place your pattern on a newspaper pad. Follow these directions to
make the Diwali lamp:

• Color the lamp: Use a brown crayon to color the exterior of
the lamp.

• Add a wick: Cut a length of yarn to glue along the broken line.

• Add oil: Use the cotton swab to spread a thin layer of vegetable oil
on the inside of the lamp.

• Light the lamp: Cut a flame shape out of tissue paper and glue to the
right end of the wick.

Extension Activity

Pair up children for a Diwali gift exchange. First, have children fold a
sheet of paper in half and then unfold it. Ask them to draw a gift for
their partner on one side of the page and write (or dictate) the name
of the gift on the other side. Then have them refold their papers and
decorate the outside to resemble a wrapped gift. Finally, invite children
to present their "gifts" to their partners.

MATERIALS

For each child:
- lamp pattern (page 171)
- newspaper pad
- brown crayon
- cotton swab

To share:
- scissors
- white yarn
- glue
- small cup of vegetable
  cooking oil
- red, yellow, and orange tissue
  paper scraps

BOOK 📖 BREAK

Diwali: Hindu Festival of Lights by June Preszler (First Facts Books,
2006). Simple text and photos introduce readers to Diwali.

Holidays Around the World: Celebrate Diwali by Deborah Heiligman
(National Geographic Children's Books, 2006). Introduces the
history, traditions, and contemporary celebration of Diwali in
different countries.

Six-Point Star

Children craft this sparkling star decoration for the Hanukkah holiday.

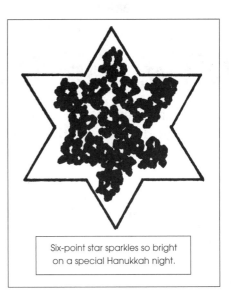

Six-point star sparkles so bright on a special Hanukkah night.

Facts to Share

Hanukkah lasts for eight nights and celebrates the victory of light over darkness. Jewish families display decorations, eat special foods, and light the menorah. In the U.S., a National Hanukkah Menorah is displayed on the Ellipse across from the White House. The nightly lighting of this menorah is televised and viewed by Jewish communities around the world.

Introducing the Activity

Share facts about Hanukkah with children, using the books listed in "Book Break" and other resources of your choice. Discuss the symbols and traditions of the holiday, including the menorah, shammash, dreidel, six-point star, and latkes. Then invite children to make these special six-point stars.

What to Do

1. Cut out the star and text box.

2. Sponge-paint the star with blue paint. Sprinkle silver glitter on the wet paint. Let the paint dry.

3. Glue the star and text box to the foil.

Extension Activity

Copy and cut out a supply of the star pattern on page 172. Write a Hanukkah-related word on each star, such as *shammash, menorah, dreidel, latke,* and *star.* (Depending on the number of stars to be used, you might use the same word on more than one star.) Review each word and discuss its meaning and how it relates to Hanukkah. Then divide the class into small groups and give each group a labeled star. Ask the groups to draw pictures that represent their words. Then help them write a sentence or two to tell about their drawings. When finished, invite the groups to share their drawings and sentences with the class.

● ● ● ● ● ● ● ● ● ● BOOK 📖 BREAK ● ● ● ● ● ● ● ● ● ●

Celebrate Chanukah by Deborah Heiligman (National Geographic Children's Books, 2006). Chanukah history and contemporary celebrations across the world are covered in this photo-illustrated book.

Hanukkah: A Counting Book in English, Hebrew, and Yiddish by Emily Sper (Cartwheel, 2003). Vibrant graphics illustrate Hanukkah customs and symbols.

● ● ● ● ● MATERIALS ● ● ● ● ●

For each child:
■ star and text patterns (page 172)
■ scissors
■ 8- by 10-inch sheet of aluminum foil (or silver foil wrapping paper)
■ glue

To share:
■ blue tempera paint mixed with a small amount of glue
■ small sponge squares
■ silver glitter

Glow, Farolito, Glow!

Children learn about a Las Posadas tradition with this special farolito.

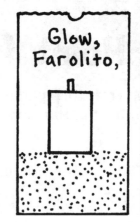

Facts to Share

Las Posadas is a nine-day celebration held in Mexico and several southwestern states in the United States. Each night, participants reenact the biblical story of Joseph and Mary's visit to Bethlehem. Symbols and traditions of Las Posadas include *peregrinos* (pilgrims), *posadas* (inns), *farolitos* (small bags with candles), *bischochitos* (sugar cookies), and *piñatas* (paper-mache containers).

Introducing the Activity

Introduce children to Las Posadas, using the books listed in "Book Break" and other resources of your choice. Discuss the activities, traditions, and common terms (see "Facts to Share") related to the holiday. Then invite children to make these unique, fold-down farolitos.

What to Do

1. Color one side of the white rectangle light brown and the other side yellow.

2. Color the bottom 3 inches of the paper bag panel light brown. Glue sand on the brown part of the panel and the brown side of the rectangle.

3. Use the marker to write "Glow, Farolito," at the top of the panel. Then write "Glow!" on the yellow square.

4. To make a lit candle, glue the yellow square along the sand line on the panel. Cut a flame shape out of the red tissue-paper square and glue it to the top of the candle.

5. Glue the rectangle over the candle with the sand side down. Glue only along the bottom to create a fold-down flap. Add a yarn "wick" to the top of the rectangle. (When closed, the flap will look like a yellow candle. When folded down, it will blend with the sand.)

MATERIALS

For each child:
- 2- by 3-inch rectangle of white construction paper
- brown and yellow crayons
- front or back panel of a white paper lunch bag
- 2-inch square of yellow construction paper
- black marker
- 1-inch square of red tissue paper
- scissors
- glue

To share:
- sand
- yarn

BOOK 📖 BREAK

Las Posadas by Jennifer Blizin Gillis (Heinemann, 2002). Photo-illustrations and simple text provide basic information about Las Posadas.

Las Posadas: An Hispanic Christmas Celebration by Diane Hoyt-Goldsmith (Holiday House, 2000). Introduces the holiday and its origins as well as related customs, foods, music, and art.

Christmas Lights

Children create this booklet to
light up the Christmas season.

Facts to Share
People around the world celebrate Christmas with worship, music,
family gatherings, and gift-giving. Traditional holiday decorations
include Nativity scenes, angels, stars, Christmas trees, and lights. In
many countries, people light candles or hang strings of light to brighten
up their homes and holiday decorations, as well as to illuminate the
long, dark nights of December.

Introducing the Activity
Use the books listed in "Book Break" to share information about how
Christmas is celebrated in different parts of the world. Point out how
people use lights to celebrate and decorate for the holiday. Then ask
children to brainstorm different ways they've seen Christmas lights
used. After sharing, invite them to make these booklets about
Christmas lights.

What to Do
1. Cut out and sequence the booklet pages. Stack them behind the
   construction-paper cover and staple along the left side.

2. Color the picture on each page. Add lights to the tree on page 2.
   Add details to make the person on page 4 resemble you.

3. Read the sentence on each page. Write (or dictate) the missing
   word to make the sentence match the picture.

4. Write "Holiday Lights" and your name on the cover. If desired,
   decorate it with crayons and glitter glue.

Extension Activity
Copy "A Christmas Sight" onto chart paper. Read the rhyme aloud
several times to teach it to children. Then invite volunteers to lead the
class in reciting the rhyme. Have them track the words with a pointer
as the class follows along. You might also have children identify the
rhyming words, examine their spelling patterns, and brainstorm other
words that rhyme with these.

MATERIALS
For each child:
- booklet pages (pages 173–174)
- scissors
- 4 ½- by 7½-inch white
  construction paper (for
  booklet cover)
- crayons
- glitter glue (optional)

To share:
- stapler

A Christmas Sight

Each little light
Shines so bright.
Oh, what a sight
On Christmas night!

BOOK 📖 BREAK

Christmas by Trudi Strain Trueit (Children's Press, 2006). Full-color
photographs fill this book about Christmas customs around the world.

Christmas Around the World by Mary D. Lankford (HarperTrophy, 1998).
Explores how Christmas is celebrated in twelve different countries.

Kinara Colors

Children learn about the colors of
Kwanzaa with this holiday kinara.

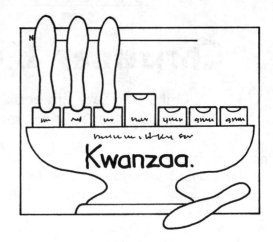

Facts to Share

Kwanzaa is a seven-day holiday during which African-American families
gather to celebrate their heritage with food, gifts, music, and dancing.
One of the highlights of the celebration is the nightly candle-lighting.
The Swahili word for candelabra is *kinara*. Candles are called *mishumaa*.
A Kwanzaa kinara holds one black, three red, and three green candles.
Black represents the face of the African people, red stands for their
blood, and green depicts the fertile land and hope for new life.

Introducing the Activity

Show children one or more pictures of a kinara with its candles in
place. (You might use pictures from the books listed in "Book Break.")
Discuss the colors of the candles and the order of their placement. Then
have children match colors to color words when they make these kinaras.

What to Do

1. Trace the word *Kwanzaa* on the kinara. Color the base of the
kinara brown.

2. Read the word on each candleholder. Lightly color the candleholder
with the matching crayon color.

3. Color three craft spoons red, three green, and one black. Each craft
spoon represents a candle.

4. Match each craft-spoon candle to the same color candleholder. Fit
the small end of the candle in the curve of the candleholder. You
can glue the candles in place, or leave them loose so that you can
match the colors over and over!

Extension Activity

Give children practice in recognizing number words. Write the words
for 1–10 on separate index cards and place in a pocket chart. Invite
children to read each word as you point to it. Repeat several times,
mixing up the order of the number words. Then teach children the
rhyme "Kwanzaa Candles." As they recite the rhyme with you, have
them hold up the corresponding number of fingers each time they
come to a number word.

BOOK 📖 BREAK

Let's Get Ready for Kwanzaa by Joanne Winne (Children's Press,
2000). This photo-illustrated book introduces readers to Kwanzaa.

My First Kwanzaa Book by Deborah Chocolate (Scholastic,
1999). Readers follow a family as they take part in Kwanzaa
activities together.

MATERIALS

For each child:
- kinara pattern (page 175)
- crayons
- 7 wooden craft spoons
- glue (optional)

Kwanzaa Candles

See the Kwanzaa candles
All in a row.
Set in the kinara,
This is how they go:
Three red, one black,
Three green stand tall.
These are mishumaa—
Seven candles in all!

New Year's Hat

Children celebrate New Year's Day
with this festive shape booklet.

Facts to Share

New Year celebrations are age-old traditions in which people say
farewell to the old year and greet the new year. In America, New Year's
Eve is a festive occasion. Partygoers watch clocks and count down to
midnight. At that hour, they throw confetti, blow horns, light fireworks,
exchange kisses, and wish all those around them a happy new year.

Introducing the Activity

Share some ways in which the new year is greeted and celebrated in
our country and other parts of the world. (You might use information
from the books listed in "Book Break.") Invite children to tell how
they celebrate New Year's Eve. Then take a poll to find out how many
children have worn New Year's party hats. Afterward, have them make
these party-hat booklets to welcome in the new year.

What to Do

1. Cut out the booklet patterns. Complete each page as described.
   cover: Write your name on the line. Color a festive design
         around the title.
   pages 1 and 2: Color the picture on each page.
   page 3: Use a pencil to draw the hands on the clock to read
         12:00. Color the clock.
   page 4: Write the old year and the new year on the lines.
   page 5: Draw a picture of yourself celebrating the New Year.

2. Sequence and stack the booklet pages behind the cover. Staple the
   booklet together at the top.

3. Glue the pompom at the top of the cover so that it resembles a
   party hat.

Extension Activity

Explain that noise-making became a New Year's tradition because it
was once believed that loud noises frightened away any bad luck
associated with the old year. Then copy the countdown rhyme, "The
New Year," onto chart paper and teach it to children. After they are
familiar with the words, invite children to stomp on bubble wrap
squares to make the sound of fireworks.

MATERIALS

For each child:
- booklet patterns
  (pages 176–177)
- scissors
- crayons and glitter crayons
- pencil
- glue
- pompom

To share:
- stapler

The New Year

Here it comes—
Midnight is near.
Here it comes—
A brand new year.

Ten, nine, eight,
Seven, six, five, four,
Three, two, one!
The New Year is here!

BOOK 📖 BREAK

New Year's Day by Dana Meachen Rau (Children's Press, 2000).
Worldwide New Year's Eve and New Year's Day customs are presented
in this photo-illustrated book.

New Year's Day by David F. Marx (Children's Press, 2000). This book
includes New Year customs from The United States, Korea, and India.

Dancing Dragon

Children greet the Chinese New Year with this expandable dragon booklet.

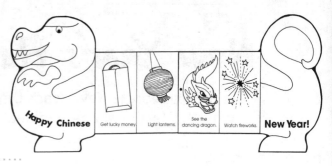

Facts to Share

In China, colorful celebrations mark the beginning of a new year. Before the new year starts, families clean their homes to get rid of bad luck. Then they observe the holiday with festivities and feasting. To encourage good fortune and prosperity, children are given money in red envelopes decorated with good luck messages. Chinese communities around the world celebrate the new year with parades featuring floats, music, and fantastic dancing dragons.

Introducing the Activity

Share information about the Chinese New Year with children, using books from "Book Break" and other resources of your choice. Explain that in the Chinese culture, dragons symbolize prosperity and long life—things everyone wishes for in the new year. Then invite children to make these foldout dragon booklets about the Chinese New Year.

What to Do

1. Color and cut out the booklet patterns.

2. Glue the pages together where indicated.

3. Accordion-fold the booklet on the lines so that the front of the dragon is on top.

4. Glue a wiggle eye to the dragon.

Extension Activity

In China, red symbolizes health, happiness, and prosperity. Red "lucky money" envelopes are given with wishes for the recipient to have all these things. Distribute index cards and red envelopes to each child in a pair. Have children write (or dictate) good luck wishes for their partners on the cards. Then have them decorate their envelopes with gold glitter glue. When the glue dries, ask children to insert their messages into their envelopes to present to their partners.

MATERIALS

For each child:
- booklet patterns (pages 178–179)
- crayons
- scissors
- glue stick
- wiggle eye

BOOK 📖 BREAK

Celebrating Chinese New Year by Diane Hoyt-Goldsmith (Holiday House, 1999). Color photographs illustrate San Francisco's Chinese New Year celebration.

Happy New Year! by Demi (Crown Books for Young Readers, 2003). Vibrant illustrations fill this book about the New Year traditions in China.

Lion Dancer: Ernie Wan's Chinese New Year by Kate Waters (Scholastic, 1999). Ernie Wan takes part in the Lion Dance during his community's Chinese New Year celebration.

Masquerade Days

Children learn about masquerade celebrations with this fun and simple booklet.

Facts to Share

Several winter celebrations are observed with dressing up in disguises, parades, and other festivities. Here are a few:

- Karneval is celebrated before the Lent fasting season. Long ago, people believed that winter could be frightened away with scary disguises and loud noises.
- Mardi Gras also is observed before Lent. Many parade and party participants wear masks and costumes to hide their true identities.
- Purim is observed after a Jewish fasting period. Along with dressing up in costumes, these celebrations include reading the biblical book of Esther, giving gifts of food, and holding beauty contests.

Introducing the Activity

Share pictures and information about various masquerade celebrations. (You might use the books listed in "Book Break.") Then point out that people long ago often wore disguises to scare away bad weather and spirits. Today disguises are worn for fun. Invite children to tell about costumes they have worn. Then have them make these booklets about disguises.

What to Do

1. Cut out the booklet patterns. Sequence and stack the pages behind the cover. Staple the booklet together along the left edge.

2. Write your name on the cover. Add hair and color the picture to represent yourself.

3. Read the text on each page and draw a picture of yourself to match it. Complete the sentence at the bottom of the page by writing (or dictating) the name of the costume shown in the picture.

Extension Activity

Copy the chant "We've Had Our Fill!" onto chart paper and teach it to children. After reciting the chant several times, have them identify the rhyming pairs (*away/stay* and *chill/fill*). Then challenge children to brainstorm other words that rhyme with each pair.

MATERIALS

For each child:
- booklet patterns (pages 180–181)
- scissors
- crayons

To share:
- stapler

We've Had Our Fill!

Winter, winter go away!
We want Spring to come and stay.
We're tired of cold and feeling the chill.
Boo! Go away winter—we've had our fill!

BOOK 📖 BREAK

It's Party Time!: A Purim Story by Jonny Zucker (Barrons Educational Series 2003). A family celebrates Purim by wearing costumes, attending a synagogue, and making plenty of noise.

Mardi Gras by Ann Heinrichs (Child's World, 2006). Discover the origins of Mardi Gras and learn about the food and activities associated with this famous festival.

Spring Eggs

Children learn about the symbolism of eggs in spring celebrations with this shape booklet.

Spring Eggs
by
Ramon

Facts to Share ....

Traditionally, eggs symbolize the new beginning, hope, joy, and regeneration that comes with Spring. People include eggs in these Spring celebrations:

- Passover: A roasted egg is one of six symbolic foods served on the Jewish Passover Seder Plate.
- Norouz: In addition to the seven traditional items placed on the Persian New Year table, a bowl of decorated eggs—one egg for each family member—may also be displayed.
- Easter: Dyed eggs were used in religious ceremonies in ancient cultures. Today, decorated eggs are a symbol of Easter and are used in a number of ways, such as in egg hunts and egg rolls.

Introducing the Activity ....

To introduce children to the Spring celebrations of Passover, Norouz, and Easter, share pictures and paraphrased text from the books listed in "Book Break." Then invite them to tell about their experiences with decorating eggs. Afterward, have children make these egg-shaped booklets.

What to Do ....

1. Cut out the booklet patterns. Sequence and stack the pages behind the cover. Then staple the booklet together on the left.

2. Complete each page as described.

cover: Write your name on the line.

page 1: Use a pencil to complete the dot-to-dot puzzle. Color the dish.

page 2: Draw an egg in the bowl for each member of your family. Color each egg and the bowl.

page 3: Draw a few Easter eggs in the basket. Decorate the eggs with bright colors and patterns.

page 4: Decorate the egg any way you like.

• • • • • • • • • • • • • • **MATERIALS** • • • • • • • •

For each child:
- booklet patterns (pages 182–184)
- scissors
- pencil
- assorted crayons (regular, glitter and fluorescent)

To share:
- stapler

• • • • • • • • • **BOOK 📖 BREAK** • • • • • • • • • • •

Celebrate Easter with Colored Eggs, Flowers, and Prayer by Deborah Heiligman (National Geographic Children's Books, 2007). Features photo-illustrations of worldwide Easter celebrations.

Celebrating Norouz: Persian New Year by Yassaman Jalali (Saman Publishing, 2003). An introduction to the Persian New Year.

Passover by David F. Marx (Children's Press, 2001). A simple introduction to the traditions and foods of Passover.

Flower Wreath

Children celebrate May Day with
this flower-filled wreath.

Facts to Share

On May 1, many countries celebrate May Day to mark the end of
winter and the arrival of spring. A traditional celebration often includes
dancing around a maypole and crowning a May Queen. Some maypoles
are decorated with flowers, wreaths, and greenery. Others have long
ribbons tied to the top, which dancers weave in interesting patterns
around the pole.

Introducing the Activity

Use the books listed in "Book Break" to show children pictures
featuring May Day activities. Explain that on May Day, many people
celebrate the arrival of spring. Fresh spring greenery and flowers are used
to decorate for the holiday. After sharing information about May Day,
invite children to make these decorative wreaths.

What to Do

1. Write your name on the back of the paper plate. Then paint the
paper plate green. Set it aside to dry.

2. Cut out the wreath label. Write *ay* on both the lines to complete
the title. Color the label light green.

3. Glue the label to the center of the plate. Sponge print colorful
flowers around the rim of the plate. Let the paint dry.

4. Add a yellow sticker dot to the center of each flower.

5. Punch a hole in the top of the paper-plate wreath. Thread the yarn
through the hole and tie the ends together to make a hanger.

6. Glue the crepe paper streamers to the bottom of the wreath.

Extension Activity

Write *May Day* on a large flower cutout. Display the flower and point
out the *ay* ending in each word. Have children brainstorm other words
that have the same word family ending (such as *say*, *way*, *play*, and
gray). Add their responses to the flower. Then invite children to make
up rhymes using words from the flower.

MATERIALS

For each child:
- 9-inch paper plate
- scissors
- pencil
- wreath label (page 136)
- glue stick
- 12-inch length of yarn
- three 8-inch lengths of crepe
  paper streamers (any color)

To share:
- green tempera paint
- paintbrushes
- shallow trays of blue, pink,
  purple, red, and orange
  tempera paint
- flower-shaped sponge painters
- yellow sticker dots
- hole punch

BOOK 📖 BREAK

Children Just Like Me: Celebrations! by Anabel Kindersley (DK Children,
1997). Explore May Day customs and activities on page 24 of this
informative book.

When Spring Comes by Robert Maass (Henry Holt, 1994). This photo-
illustrated book features all the things that make spring so special.

Bilingual Piñata

Children learn about Cinco de Mayo
with this bilingual lift-the-flap piñata.

Facts to Share

On the Fifth of May, Cinco de Mayo is observed in Mexico and parts
of the United States that have large Mexican-American communities.
The celebration commemorates Mexico's defeat over the French army
in the Battle of Puebla, which was fought on May 5, 1862. Parades,
piñatas, music, dancing, traditional Mexican foods, and fireworks are all
part of the festivities. Cinco de Mayo celebrations often end with joyous
shouts of *Viva Mexico!*

Introducing the Activity

Display pictures and share information about Cinco de Mayo. (You
might use the books listed in "Book Break.") Encourage children to also
share what they know about this holiday. Then write these Spanish
and English word pairs on chart paper: *Viva Mexico!*/Long live Mexico!,
cinco/five, *danza*/dance, *fiesta*/party, *Mayo*/May, and *bandas*/bands. Review
each word pair with children. Then invite them to make these bilingual
lift-the-flap piñatas.

What to Do

1. Cut out the piñata patterns.

2. Write your name on the center of the piñata. Then color the entire
piñata red and each flap pattern light green.

3. Place each flap on the corresponding point on the piñata, matching
the symbols at the end of each point. Glue each flap to the piñata
where indicated so that it can be lifted to reveal the word underneath.

4. Read the English word on each point on the piñata. Then lift the
flap to read the corresponding Spanish word.

Extension Activity

Use a red marker to write the Spanish words featured on the piñata on
separate index cards. Write the matching English word in green on
another set of cards. Mix up the cards and place them in a pocket chart.
If desired, provide a completed piñata for self-checking purposes.
Then invite children to match the Spanish and English word cards.

MATERIALS

For each child:
- piñata patterns
  (pages 184–185)
- scissors
- red and green crayons
- glue stick

BOOK 📖 BREAK

Cinco de Mayo by Mary Dodson Wade (Children's Press, 2003).
This book features colorful photographs and simple explanations
of the holiday.

Cinco de Mayo: Day of Mexican Pride by Amanda Doering
(Capstone Press, 2006). Includes colorful photos and simple
explanations about the history and traditions of Cinco de Mayo.

Fish Flyer

Children learn about Children's Day in
Japan with this paper-bag windsock.

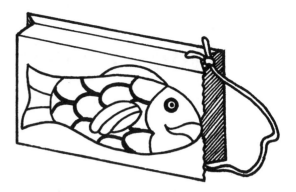

Facts to Share
Children's Day, a national holiday in Japan, is dedicated to celebrating
the health and happiness of all children. Children's Day falls on May 5,
which was traditionally celebrated with a festival for boys. On this day,
families display a carp flag or streamer for each child in the family.
The carp, a fish that swims against the current, symbolizes the wish for
children to be strong and successful like the fish itself.

Introducing the Activity
Introduce children to Children's Day, using pictures and paraphrased
text from *Japanese Children's Day and the Obon Festival* by Dianne M.
MacMillan (see "Book Break") or information from your own research.
Then discuss the symbol of the carp in this holiday celebration. Point
out that a carp must be strong and determined to swim successfully
against the current. Explain that in Japan, parents wish this same kind
of strength and success for their own children. Then invite children to
make these carp windsocks to celebrate Children's Day.

What to Do
1. Cut out the fish and text box. Set the text box aside for later use.

2. Use glitter crayons to trace the scales and other lines on the fish.
Paint the fish with a watercolor paint of your choice. Let the
paint dry.

3. Stick the black sticker dot over the fish's eye. Glue a wiggle eye on
top of the dot.

4. Cut off the bottom of the paper bag. Glue the fish to one side of
the bag.

5. Write (or dictate) an ending to the sentence on the text box.
Write your name on the line at the bottom. Glue the text box
to the other side of the bag.

6. Open the bag and punch a hole in each side near the top. Tie
each end of the yarn to a hole to create a hanger.

MATERIALS

For each child:
- fish and text patterns
  (page 186)
- scissors
- glitter crayons
- black sticker dot
- wiggle eye
- glue
- paper lunch bag
- pencil
- 24-inch length of yarn
- crayons

To share:
- watercolor paints
- hole punch

BOOK 📖 BREAK

A to Zen: A Book of Japanese Culture by Ruth Wells (Simon &
Schuster Children's Publishing, 1992). This exploration of Japanese
culture focuses on one topic for each letter of the alphabet.

Japanese Children's Day and the Obon Festival by Dianne M. MacMillan
(Enslow Publishers, Inc., 1997). Japanese-American families celebrate
Children's Day with games, crafts, and plays.

Happy Birthday!

Children learn about birthday traditions in different countries with this easy-to-read booklet.

Facts to Share

People around the world celebrate birthdays in different ways. Here are a few birthday traditions from different countries:

- China: Noodles are often served at a birthday celebration. The long noodles represent long life.
- Israel: The birthday child wears a crown made of leaves or flowers and sits in a decorated chair. Guests dance and sing around the chair.
- Mexico: The blindfolded birthday child swings a stick to break open a paper-mache piñata. Guests share the goodies that spill out of the piñata.
- India: The birthday child wears new clothes. If the birthday is on a school day, he or she brings chocolates to share with classmates.
- United States: Guests sing a birthday song and present the birthday child with a decorated cake topped with candles representing his or her age.

Introducing the Activity

Invite children to tell about how they celebrate birthdays. Then share how children in other countries celebrate. (You might use information from "Facts to Share" and the books from "Book Break.") Afterward, have children make these booklets about birthday traditions around the world.

What to Do

1. Cut out the booklet patterns. Complete each page as described.

cover: Glue on the title. Color the picture.

page 1: Glue on the bowl. Glue yarn above the bowl to represent noodles.

page 2: Glue on the crown. Draw facial features and color the picture.

page 3. Glue the label on the piñata and color the picture.

page 4: Glue on the chocolates. Color the chocolates light brown. If desired, trace the lines on them with glitter glue.

page 5: Color the cake and add candles.

2. Sequence and stack the booklet pages behind the cover. Staple the booklet together along the left side.

MATERIALS

For each child:
- booklet patterns (pages 187–189)
- scissors
- glue stick
- crayons
- yellow yarn

To share:
- glitter glue (optional)
- stapler

BOOK 📖 BREAK

Celebrating Birthdays in China by Cheryl L. Enderlein (Capstone Press, 1998). Introduces the parties, food, and presents found at Chinese birthday celebrations.

The World of Birthdays by Paula S. Wallace (Gareth Stevens Publishing, 2002). Explores birthday celebrations around the world, including Mexico, India, and the United States.

Cakes and Candles

Children learn about cakes and candles and then create a cute booklet about baking a cake all their own.

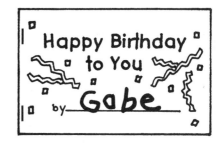

Facts to Share

It is believed that celebrating birthdays with cakes and candles originated in ancient Greece. The Greeks made moon-shaped cakes to honor their moon goddess. They added candles to make their cakes glow like the moon. The tradition of making a wish when blowing out birthday candles stems from the belief that smoke from the candles carried wishes to the heavens.

Introducing the Activity

Invite children to tell about the kinds of birthday cakes they have seen or enjoyed during birthday celebrations. Then share facts about birthday cakes and candles from "Facts to Share." Afterward, talk about the steps to follow when baking a cake. Finally, have children create these booklets about birthday cakes. (Later, you might share cake pictures and even help children make one of the cakes from a book listed in "Book Break.")

What to Do

1. Cut out the booklet patterns. Complete each page as described.

cover: Write your name on the line. Glue on colorful crinkle strips and confetti.

page 1: Color the bowl. Glue a little flour to the inside of it.

page 2: Glue the cake pan to the oven rack. Color the outside of the pan black and the inside the color of cake batter. Then glue only the bottom edge of the oven door to the oven to create a fold-down flap.

page 3: Color the cake the color of your favorite frosting.

page 4: Decorate the cake. Draw the number of candles you will need on your next birthday cake.

2. Sequence and stack the booklet pages behind the cover. Staple the booklet together along the left side.

MATERIALS

For each child:
■ booklet patterns
  (pages 190–192)
■ scissors
■ glue
■ crayons

To share:
■ crinkle paper strips in
  different colors
■ glitter confetti
■ flour
■ stapler

BOOK 📖 BREAK

The easy-to-make cake recipes in these books feature color photos and step-by-step decorating directions.

Quick & Easy Kids' Cakes: 50 Great Cakes for Children of All Ages by Sara Lewis (Hamlyn, 2006).

Bake and Make Amazing Cakes by Elizabeth MacLeod (Kids Can Press, Ltd., 2001).

Easy Cut-Up Cakes for Kids by Melissa Barlow (Gibbs Smith, 2007).

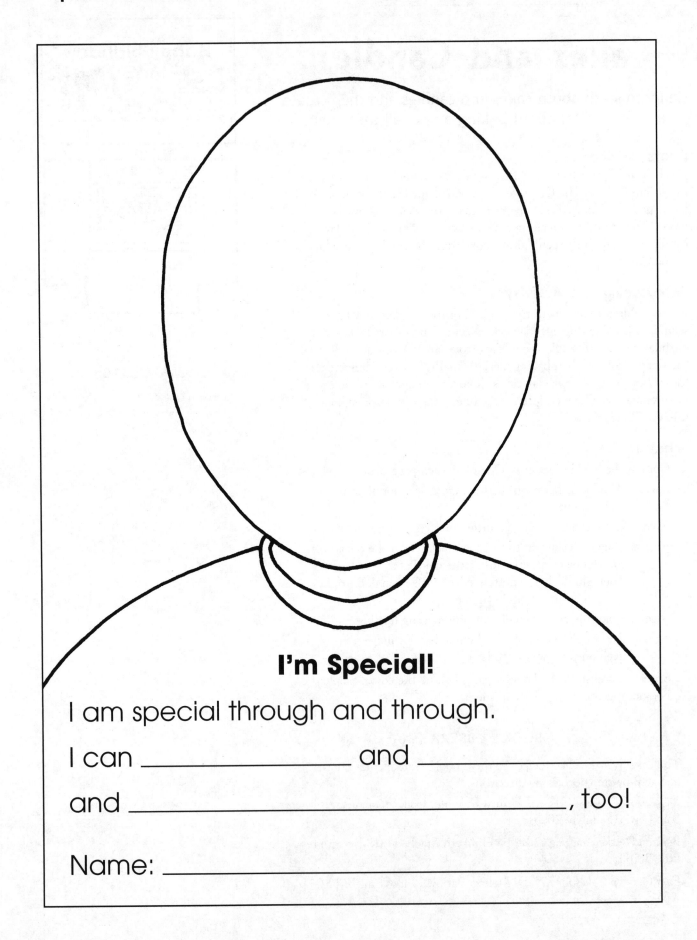

I'm Special!

I am special through and through.

I can _____ and _____

and _____, too!

Name: _____

Working Together at Home

by _____

Who sweeps?

1

Who washes dishes?

2

Who picks up?

3

Who cleans?

4

Who helps?
I do!

5

"Cooperation Quilt" Pattern

Name: _____

_____

is in our school community.

Staple flap here.

How to Care for

The Parade!

by _____

A
wagon.

1

A
bicycle.

2

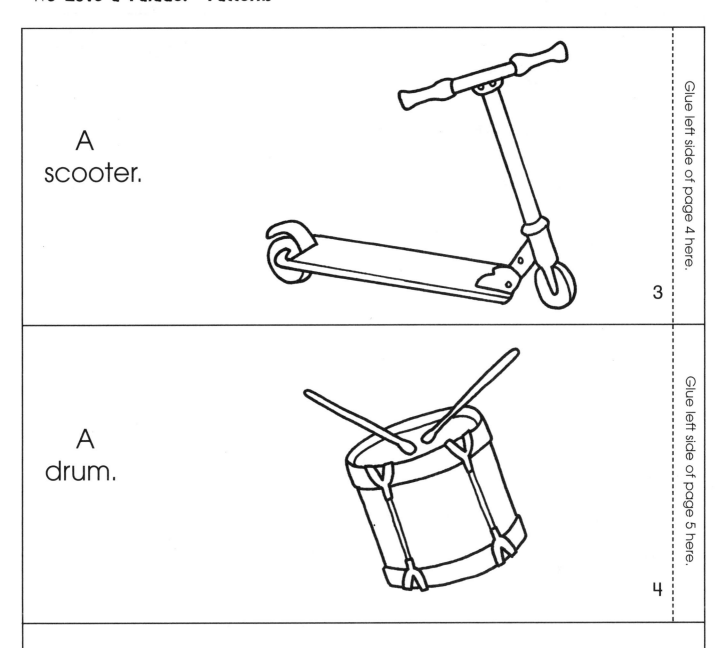

A
scooter.

Glue left side of page 4 here.

3

A
drum.

Glue left side of page 5 here.

4

I'm in the parade.
Here I come!

5

Signs Around the Neighborhood

by _____

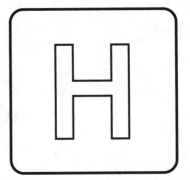 blue

hospital

1

 green

LIBRARY

library

2

 blue

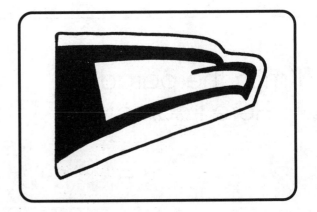

post office

3

yellow

FIRE STATION

fire station

4

blue

POLICE

police station

5

yellow

school

6

brown

PARK

park

7

What's for Sale at the Grocery Store?

by _____

This is what
I would buy:

_____

Glue bag square here.

Fast Food Order Pad

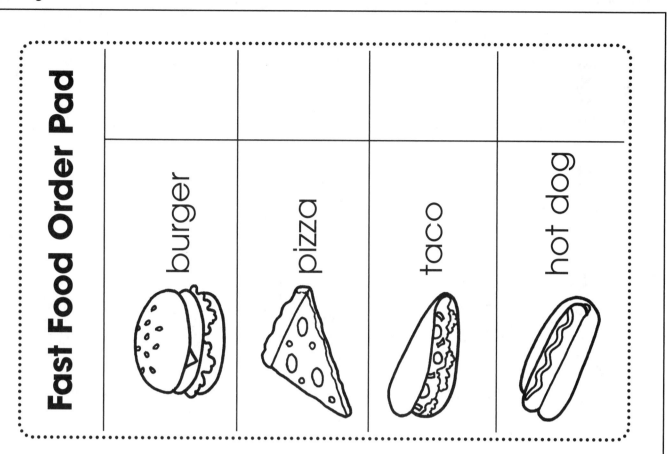

burger

pizza

taco

hot dog

Fast Food Restaurant Menu

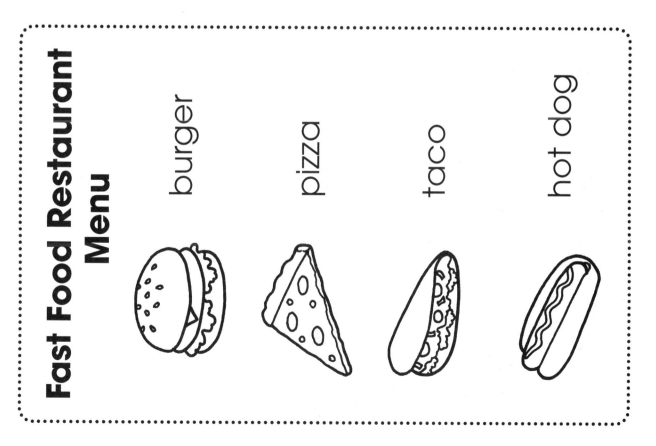

burger

pizza

taco

hot dog

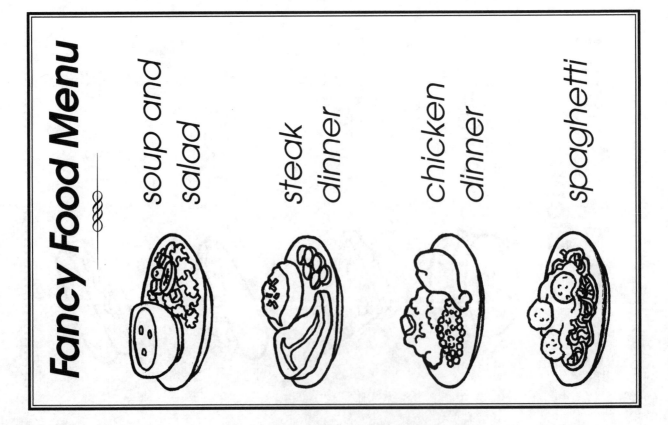

Fancy Food Order Pad

| soup and salad |
| steak dinner |
| chicken dinner |
| spaghetti |

Fancy Food Menu

soup and salad

steak dinner

chicken dinner

spaghetti

I take the

_____ home.

I choose

a _____.

I check out

the _____.

I return the

_____ to the library.

When I need a relaxing day,

I like to go to _____

for fun or play!

by _____

A
Doctor . . .

Staple pages here.

then gives me a prize!

4

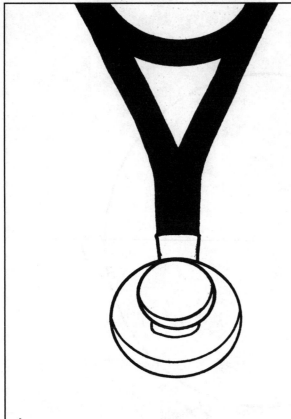

by _____

listens to my heart,

1

looks in my eyes,

2

checks my nose and ears,

3

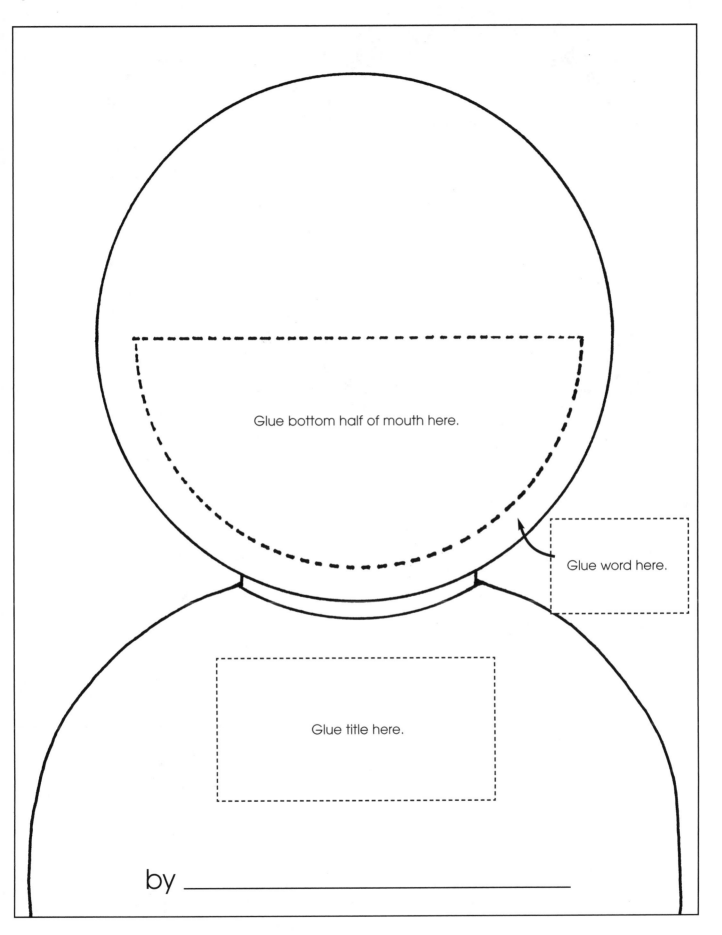

Glue bottom half of mouth here.

Glue word here.

Glue title here.

by _____

"Open Wide!" Patterns

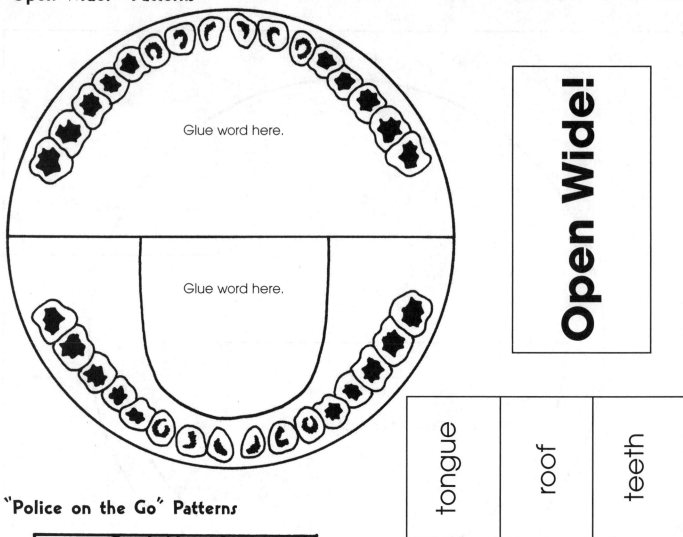

Glue word here.

Glue word here.

Open Wide!

tongue	roof	teeth

"Police on the Go" Patterns

Police on the Go

legs

police sign

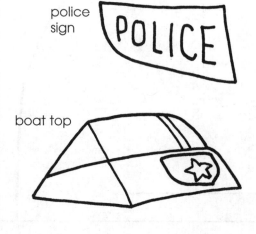
boat top

wheel

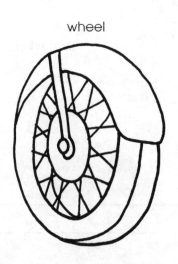

police officer

Glue title here.

by _____

Police
on their feet,
keeping us
safe,

Glue legs here.

I

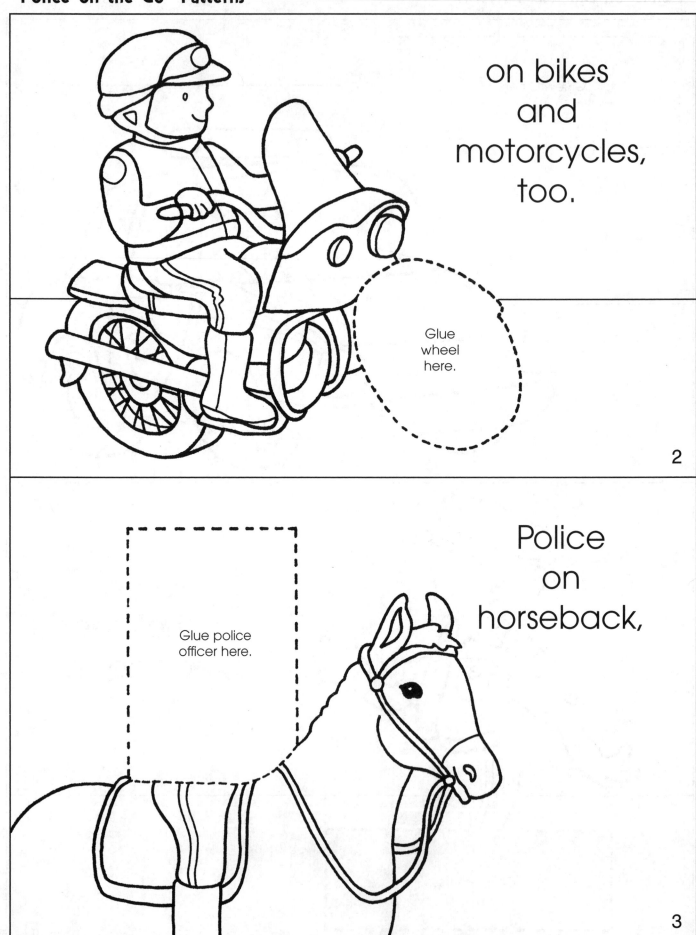

on bikes
and
motorcycles,
too.

Glue
wheel
here.

2

Police
on
horseback,

Glue police
officer here.

3

and flying
through
the
air,

4

on the go
for me
and you!

5

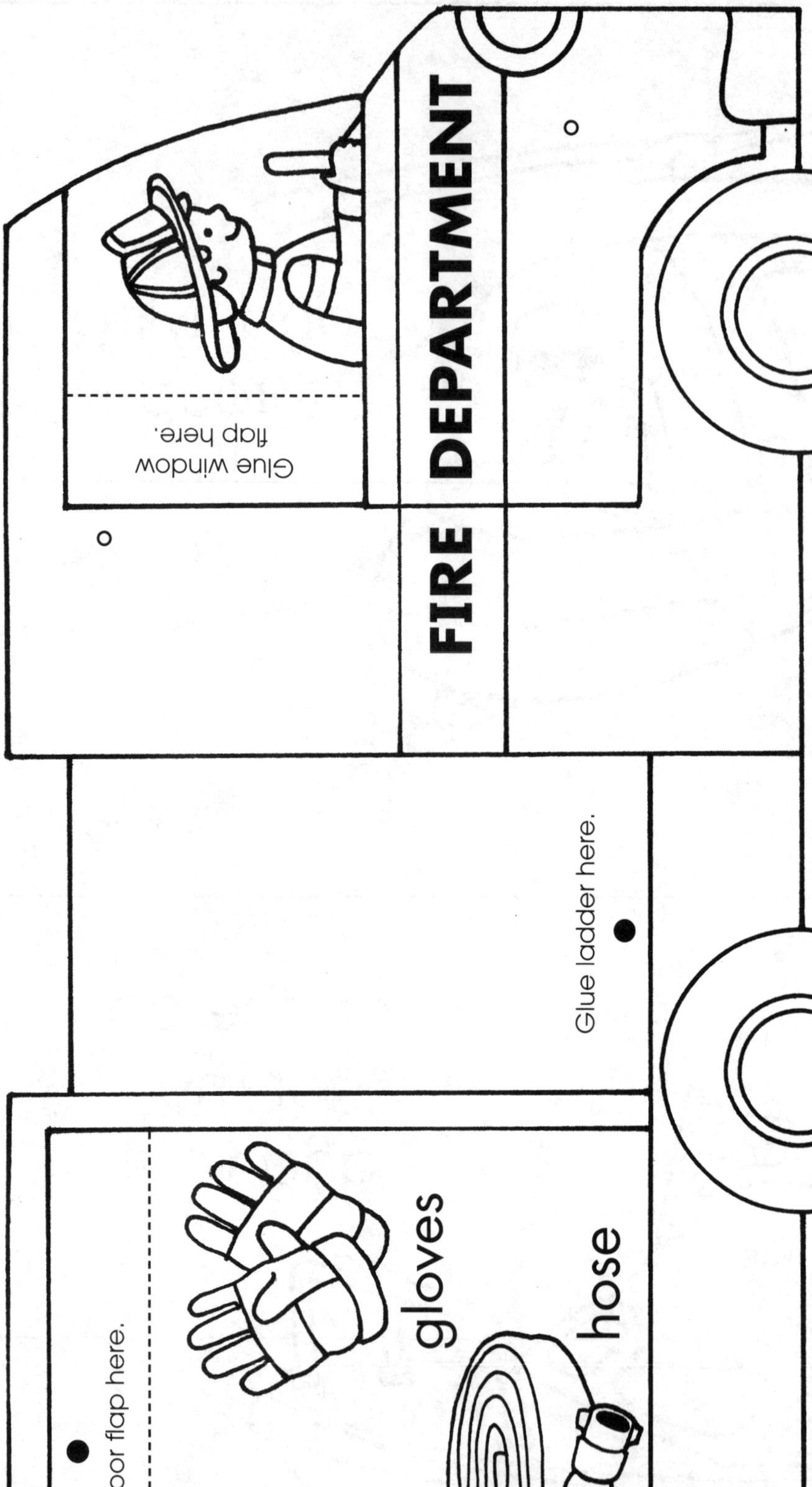

fire truck

Glue window
flap here.

FIRE DEPARTMENT

Glue ladder here.

light wheel

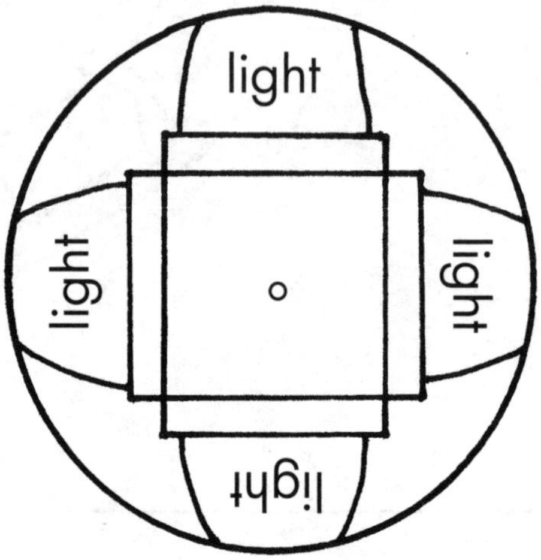

light

light

light

light

siren wheel

Glue door flap here.

gloves

hose

ax

Whoo! Whoo!

siren

siren

Whoo! Whoo!

"Fire Trucks at Work" Patterns

door flap

ladder

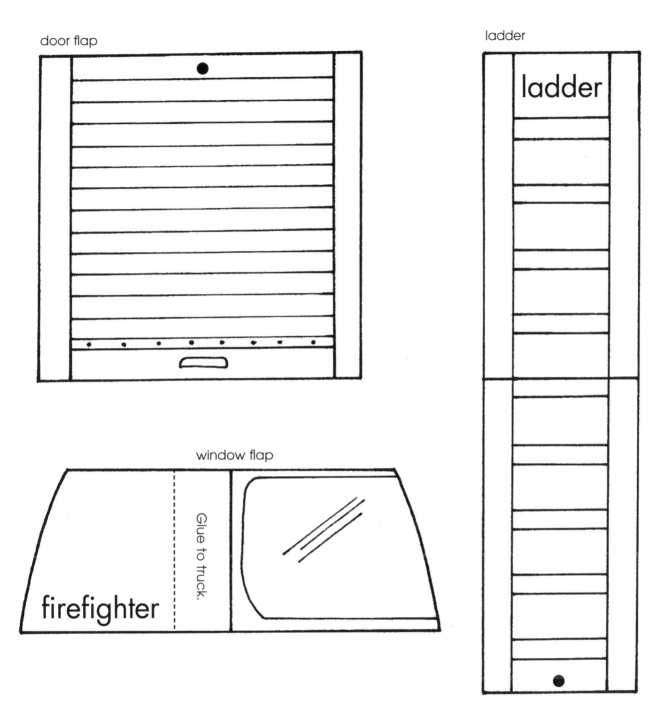

ladder

window flap

Glue to truck.

firefighter

mailbox

lid

name

_____'s class

MAIL

"It's Trash Day!" Patterns

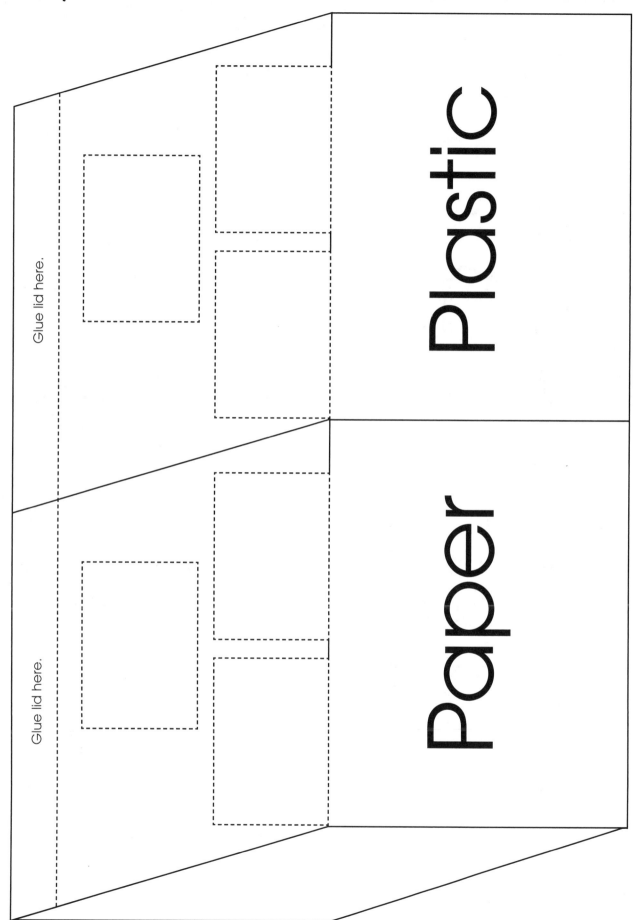

Glue lid here.

Glue lid here.

Plastic

Paper

lids

pictures

Recycle

Recycle

"Just Passing By" Pattern

Name: _____

Land Transportation Survey

car	bus	truck	bike	motorcycle	other

Traffic Signs

by _____

3

ONE WAY

1

4

YIELD

2

5

"Rules of the Road" Patterns

6

7

BIKE ROUTE

8

EXIT

9

STOP

10

Go, Boat, Go!

by _____

Go, rowboat, go!

1

Go, sailboat, go!

2

"Go, Boat, Go!" Patterns

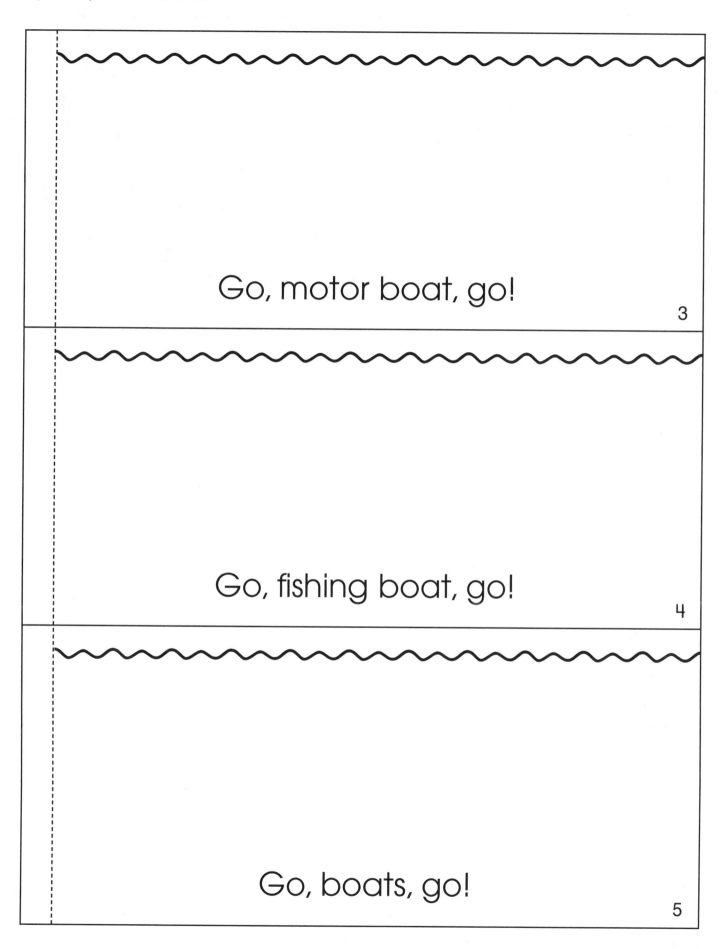

Go, motor boat, go!

3

Go, fishing boat, go!

4

Go, boats, go!

5

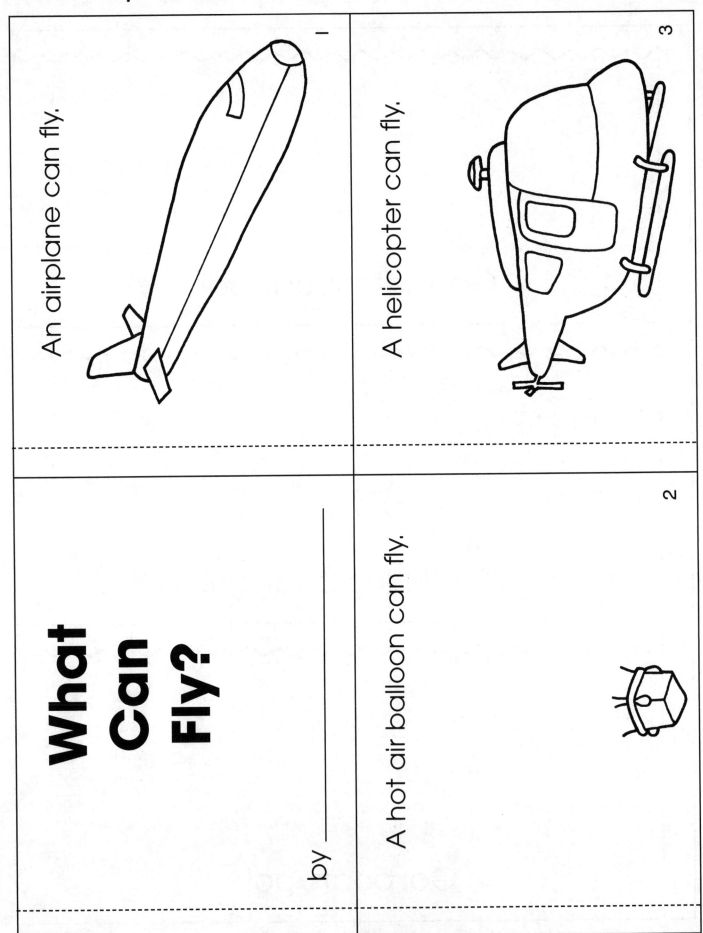

1

An airplane can fly.

3

A helicopter can fly.

What Can Fly?

by _____

2

A hot air balloon can fly.

Glue page 2 here.

and by air.

3

I can travel by land,

1

Vehicles

can take

_____

everywhere!

4

by water,

2

"Thank You, Workers!" Pattern

Thank you, ______________

for working so hard.

Thank you
for doing
your best.

I offer you my hand
this Labor Day—
a day to
relax and rest!

Signed,

____

Columbus Sets Sail

by _____

Three ships sailed.

1

Glue flap 2a here.

Day

and night.

2

Glue flap 3a here.

Good weather

and bad.

3

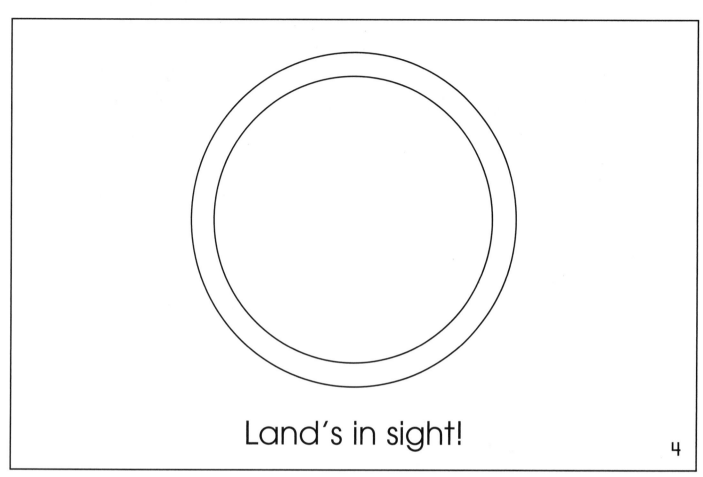

Land's in sight!

4

flap 2a   flap 3a

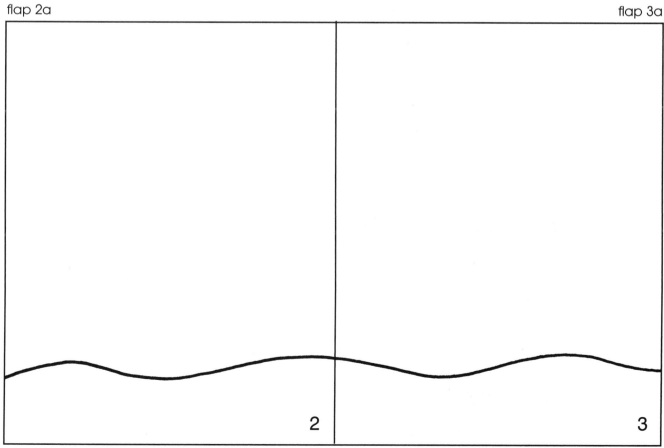

2

3

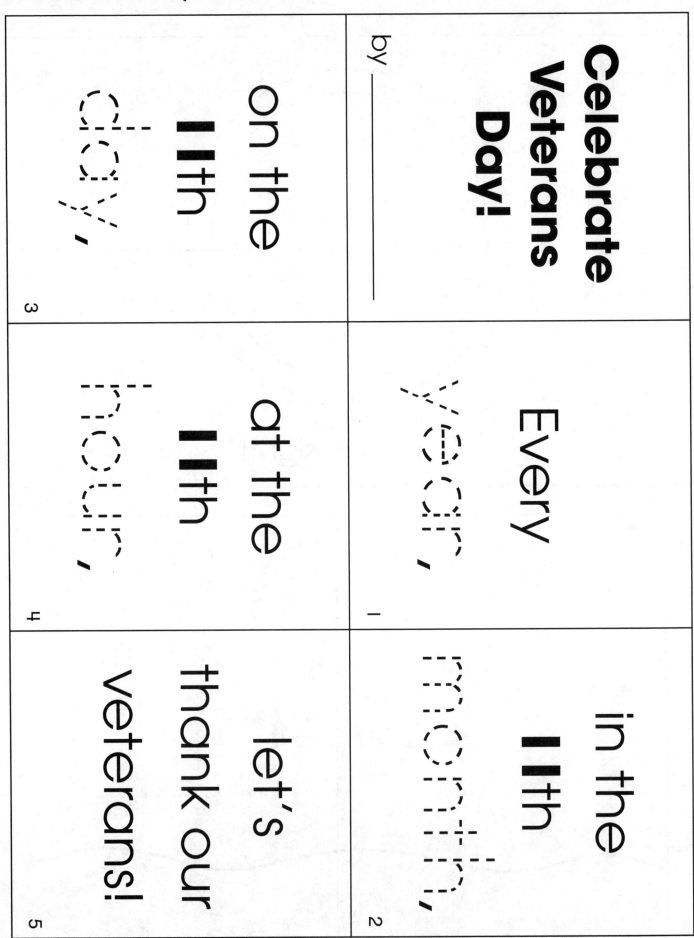

Celebrate Veterans Day!

by _____

Every year,

in the 11th month,

on the 11th day,

at the 11th hour,

let's thank our veterans!

1

2

3

4

5

"Thanksgiving Turkey" Patterns

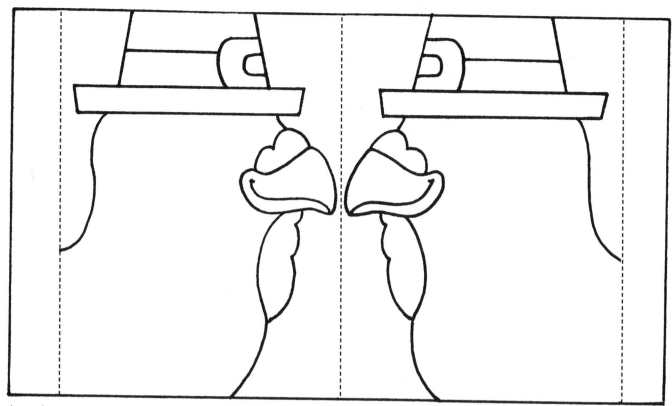

head

wings

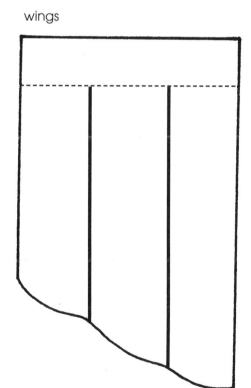
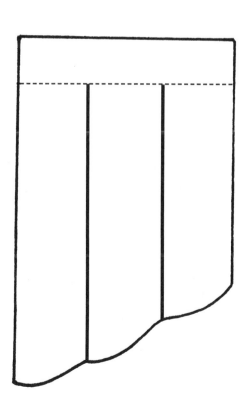

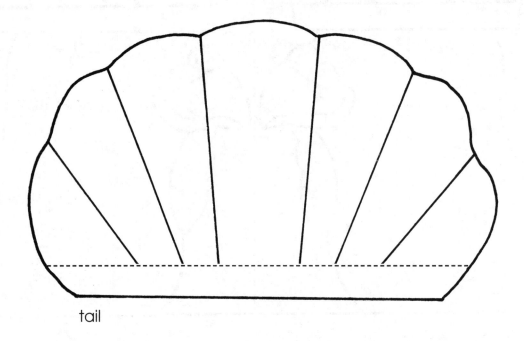

tail

My favorite Thanksgiving food is _____

_____.

I'm thankful for _____

_____.

My favorite Thanksgiving activity is _____

_____.

My favorite Thanksgiving memory is _____

_____.

120

Who was

our

first

President?

1

Who is

the

Father of

Our Country?

3

Whose

picture is on

the

one-dollar bill?

5

Whose

birthday

is

February 22?

7

George
Washington!

2

George
Washington!

4

George
Washington!

6

George
Washington!

8

Whose hand recycles paper?

Whose hand recycles cardboard?

Whose hand recycles plastic?

Whose hand recycles cans?

My hand recycles!

can

title box

Whose Hand Recycles?

by _____

"Memorial Poppies" Patterns

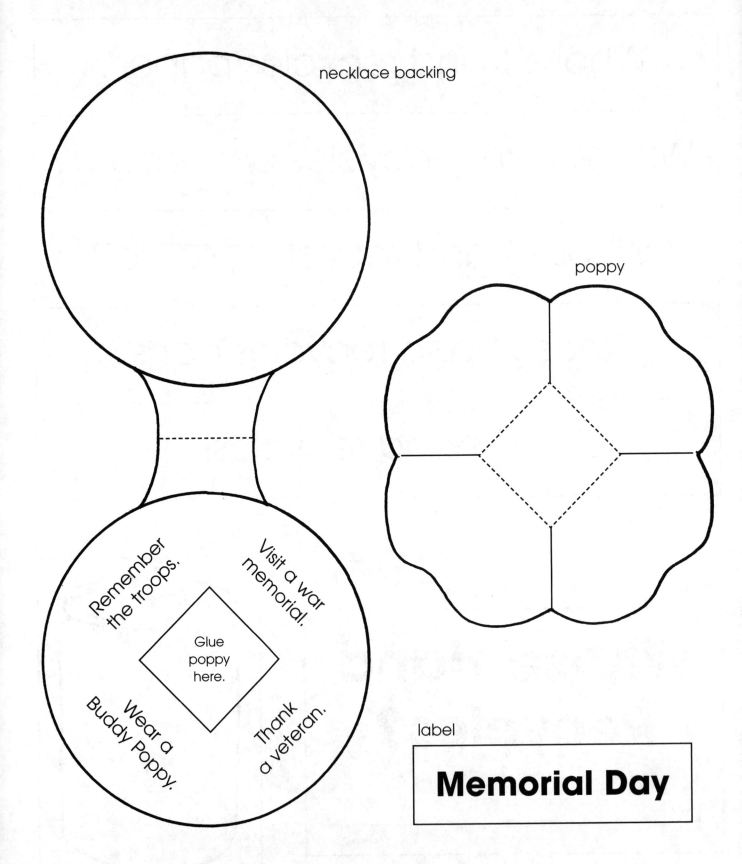

necklace backing

poppy

Remember the troops.

Visit a war memorial.

Glue poppy here.

Wear a Buddy Poppy.

Thank a veteran.

label

Memorial Day

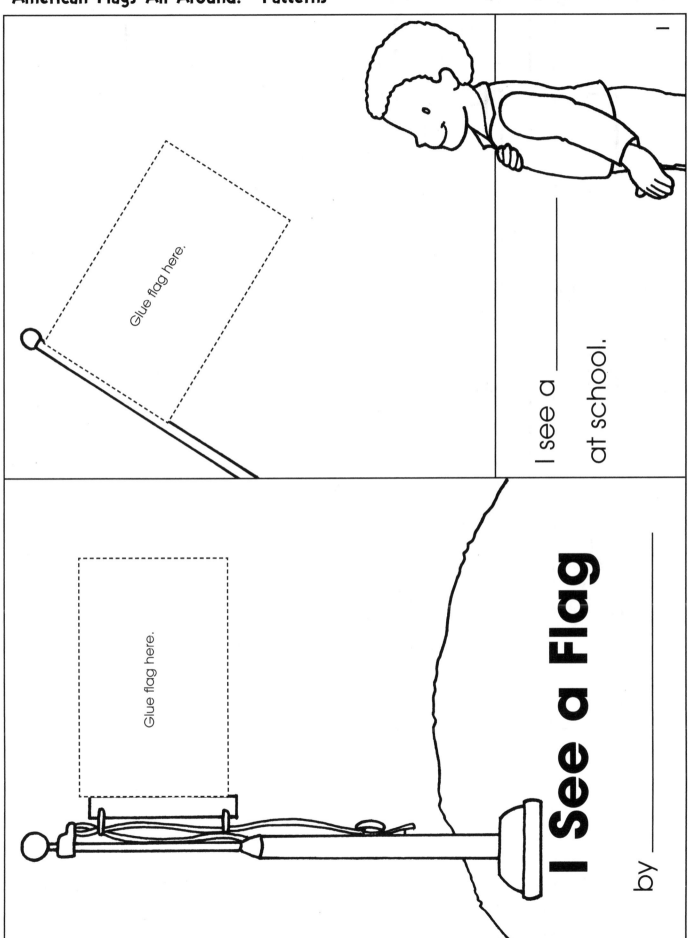

Glue flag here.

I see a ——— at school.

Glue flag here.

I See a Flag

by ———

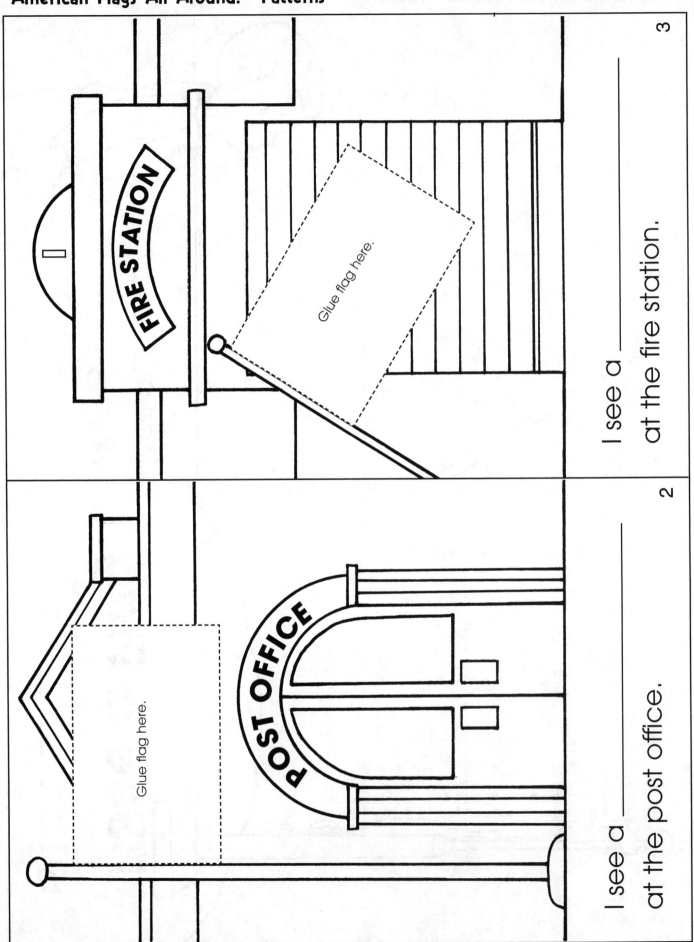

FIRE STATION

Glue flag here.

3

I see a _____
at the fire station.

2

POST OFFICE

Glue flag here.

I see a _____
at the post office.

"American Flags All Around!" Patterns

flags

Glue flag here.

A parade! I see lots of _____.

4

"Hooray for Independence Day!" Patterns

Glue page 2 here.

Glue page 3 here.

1

2

Bang the drum.

Pack a picnic.

Wave the flag.

Name _____

Hooray!

Shout hooray!

3

drum

picnic basket

Watch the fireworks. It's Independence Day!

flag

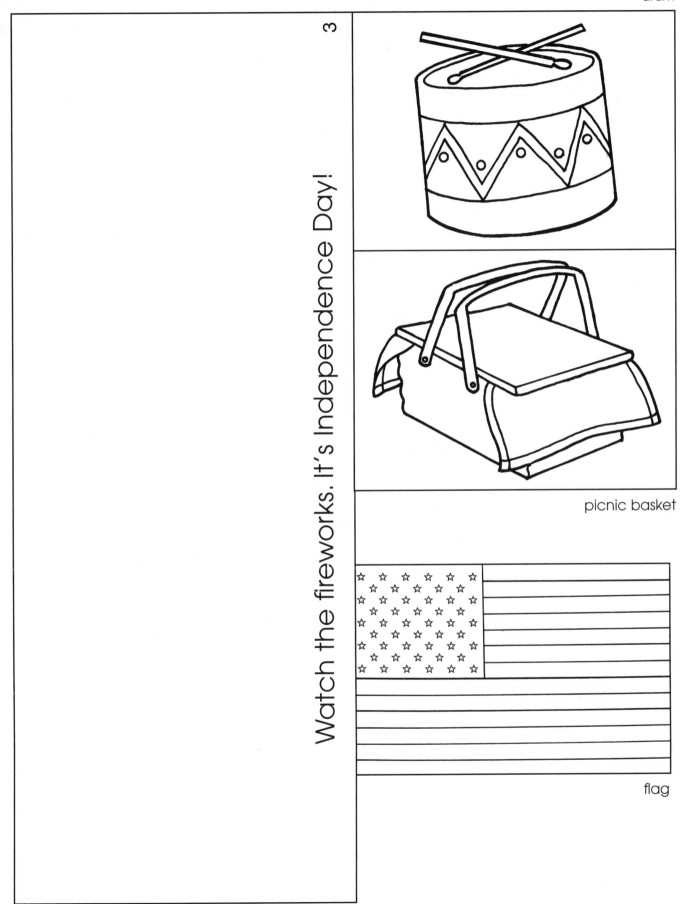

Name _____

The Pilgrims sailed on the Mayflower.

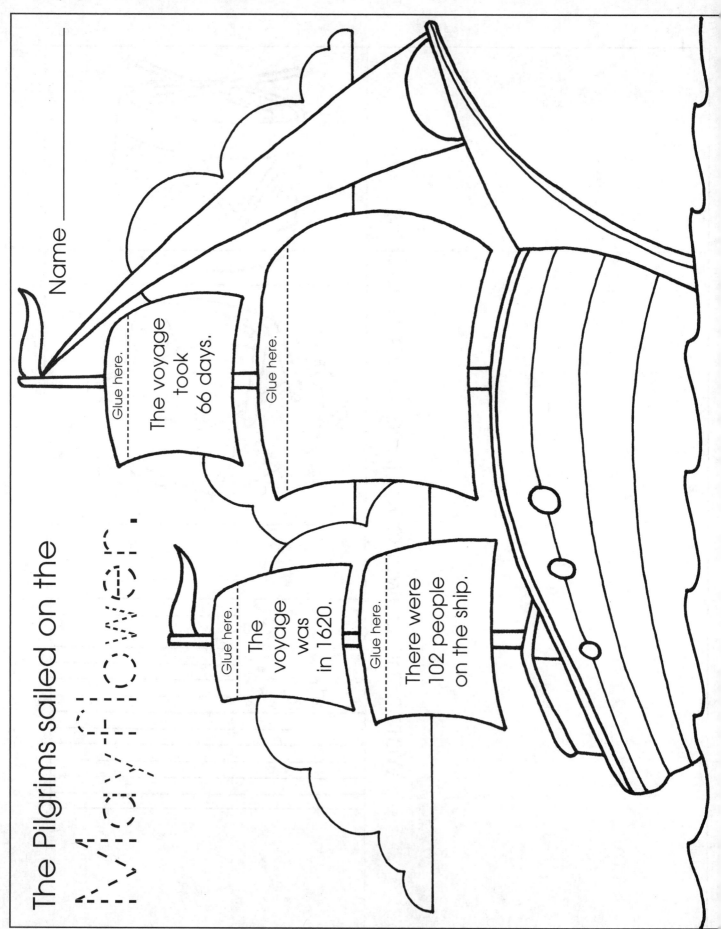

Glue here.

The voyage took 66 days.

Glue here.

Glue here.

The voyage was in 1620.

Glue here.

There were 102 people on the ship.

130

"Voyage to America" Patterns

What happened on the voyage?

How long did the voyage last?

What year was the voyage?

How many people were on the ship?

"Picture Pouches" Patterns

pumpkin	beans	corn
home	canoe	bag

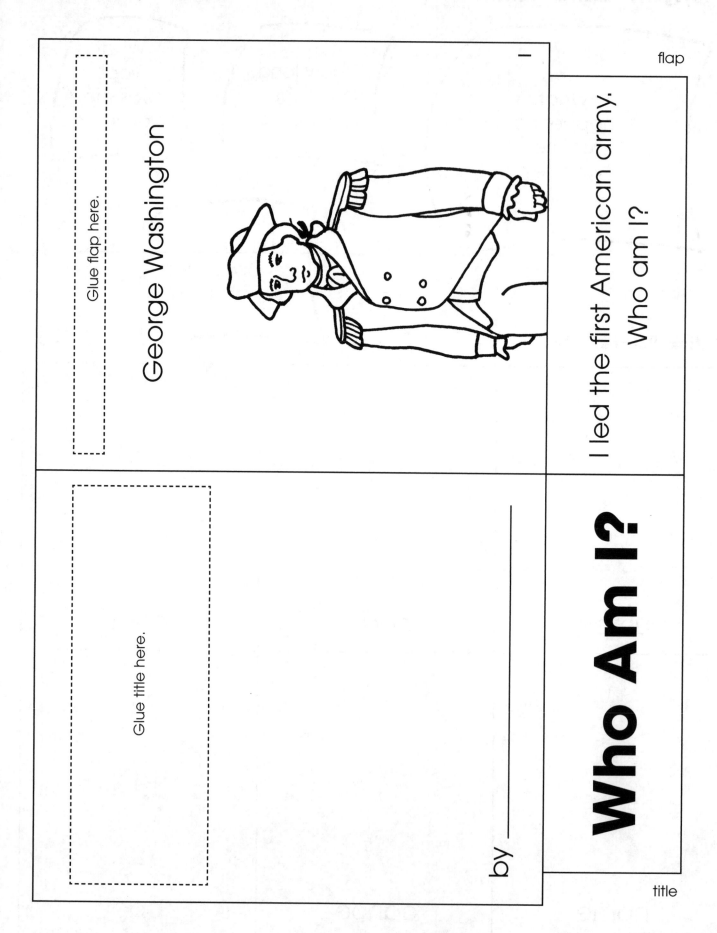

flap

Glue flap here.

George Washington

I led the first American army.
Who am I?

Glue title here.

Who Am I?

by _____

title

"Who Am I?" Patterns

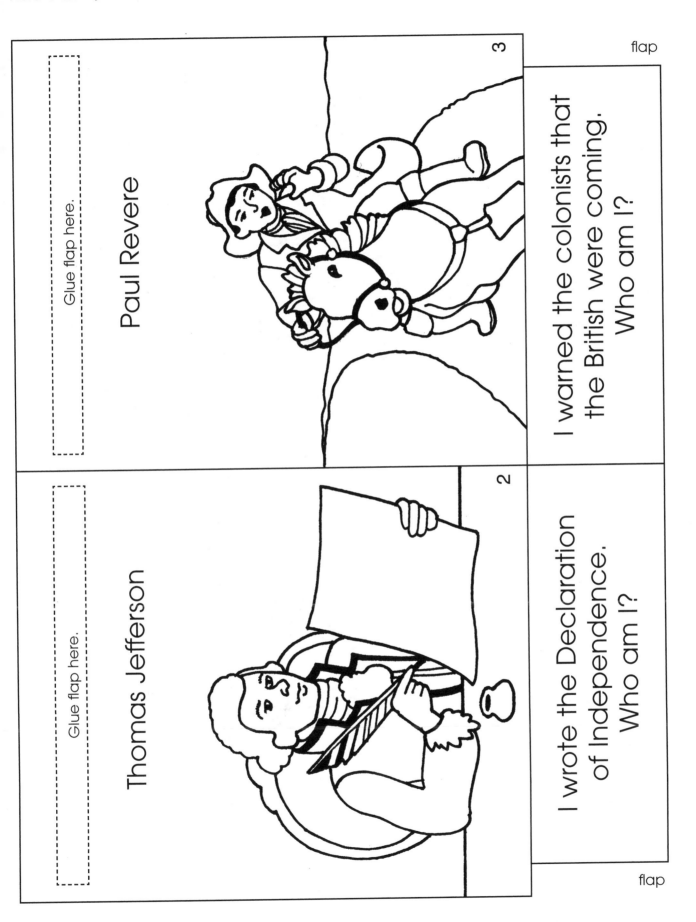

Glue flap here.

Paul Revere

3

flap

I warned the colonists that the British were coming. Who am I?

Glue flap here.

Thomas Jefferson

2

I wrote the Declaration of Independence. Who am I?

flap

Glue flap here.

John Hancock

I was the first person to sign the Declaration of Independence. Who am I?

5

flap

Glue flap here.

Betsy Ross

I sewed the first American flag. Who am I?

4

flap

What will _____ pack in the wagon?

Glue wagon top here.

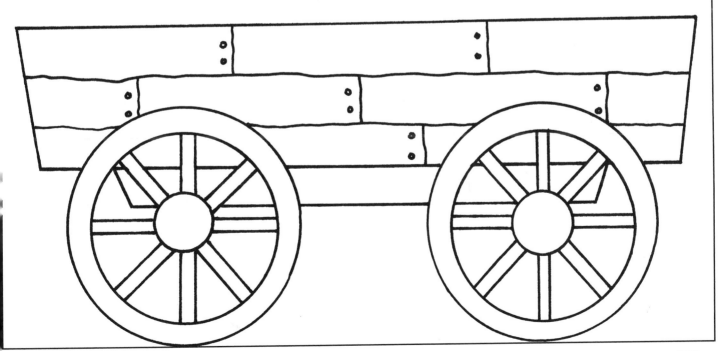

"Wagons Ho!" Patterns

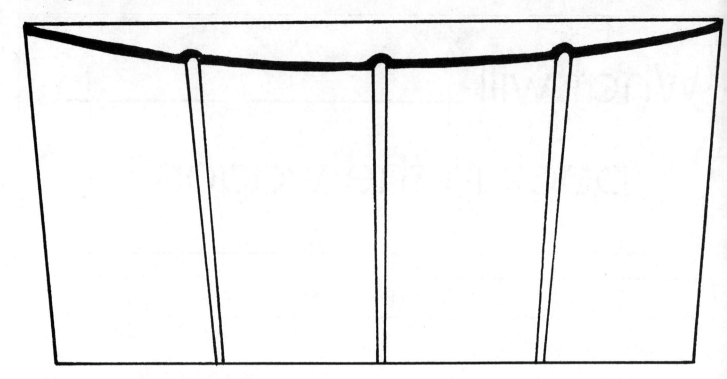

"Flower Wreath" Pattern

I Came to America!

by _____

I came to America for

_____

_____.

Name: _____

When Did People Use It?

Then	Now

These things were used long ago.

These things are used now.

quill pen	ball-point pen	wagon wheel	rubber tire	corn-husk doll	plastic doll

Glue flag here.

Glue title here.

Glue page 1 here.

by _____

Our flag has three colors.

red

white

blue

Glue page 2 here.

1

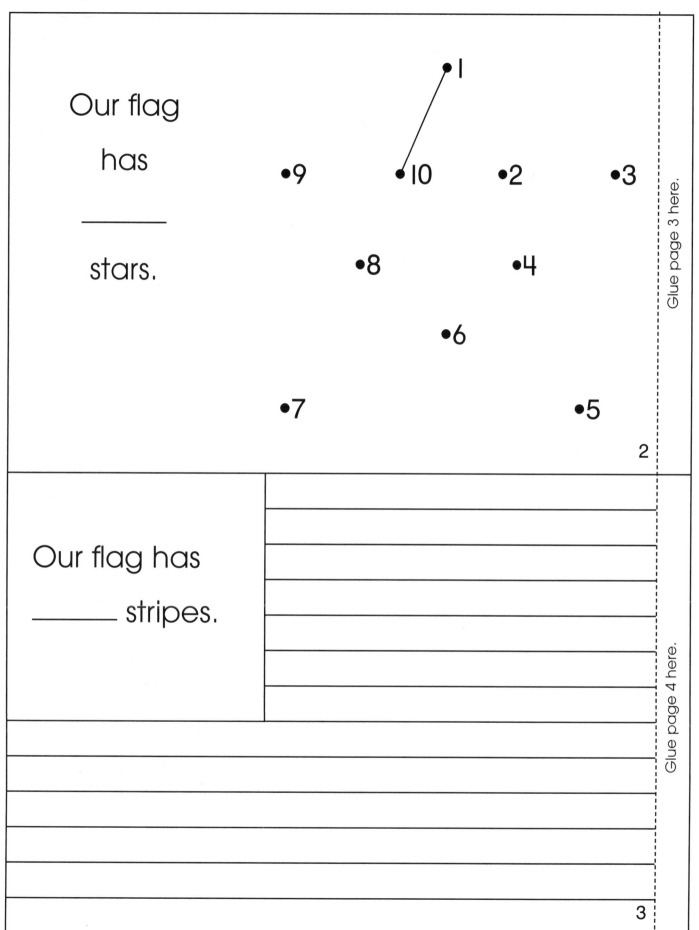

Our flag

has

_____

stars.

•9   •10   •2   •3

•8   •4

•6

•7   •5

2

Our flag has

_____ stripes.

3

I'm proud to be an American!

4

flag

title

The Liberty Bell

by _____

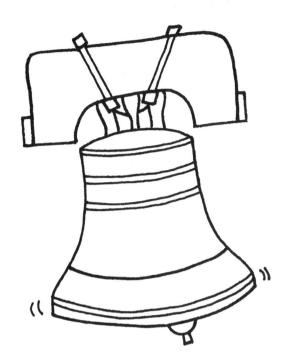

The Liberty Bell rang to celebrate freedom. 1

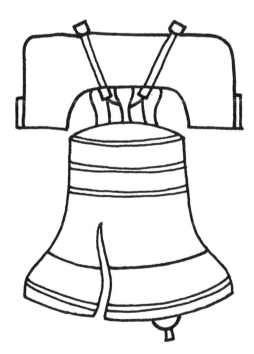

One day, the Liberty Bell cracked! 2

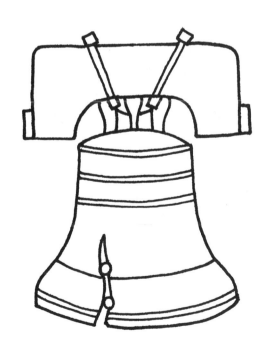

Today, the Liberty Bell is a symbol of freedom. 3

"The National Bird" Patterns

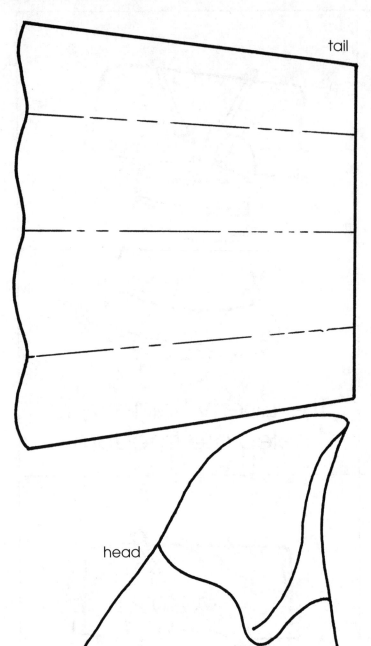

tail

The bald eagle is a national symbol.

The bald eagle stands for strength.

The bald eagle stands for freedom.

The bald eagle _____
_____
_____.

sentence strips

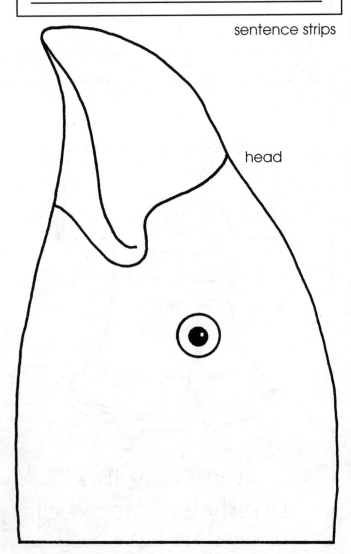

head   head

cover

Who Stands Tall?

by _____

Can you guess who
stands so tall?
The Statue of Liberty—
freedom for all!

5

Here is the torch.

1

Here is the crown.

2

Here is the tablet.

3

Here is the gown.

4

"Our Patriotic Uncle" Patterns

"The President's Home" Patterns

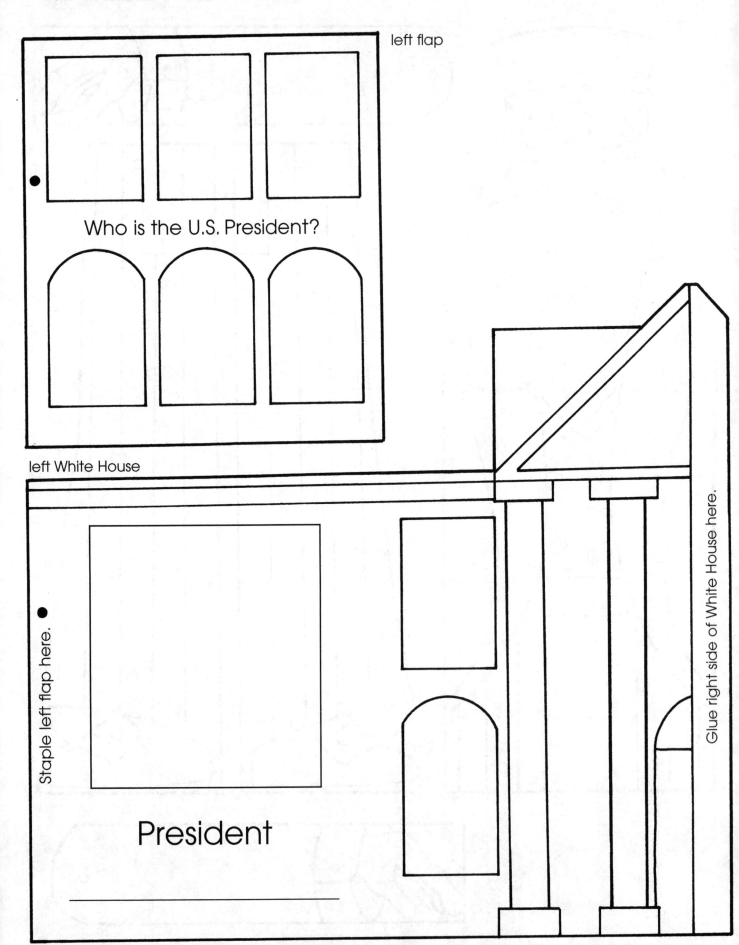

left flap

Who is the U.S. President?

left White House

Staple left flap here.

President

_____

Glue right side of White House here.

"The President's Home" Patterns

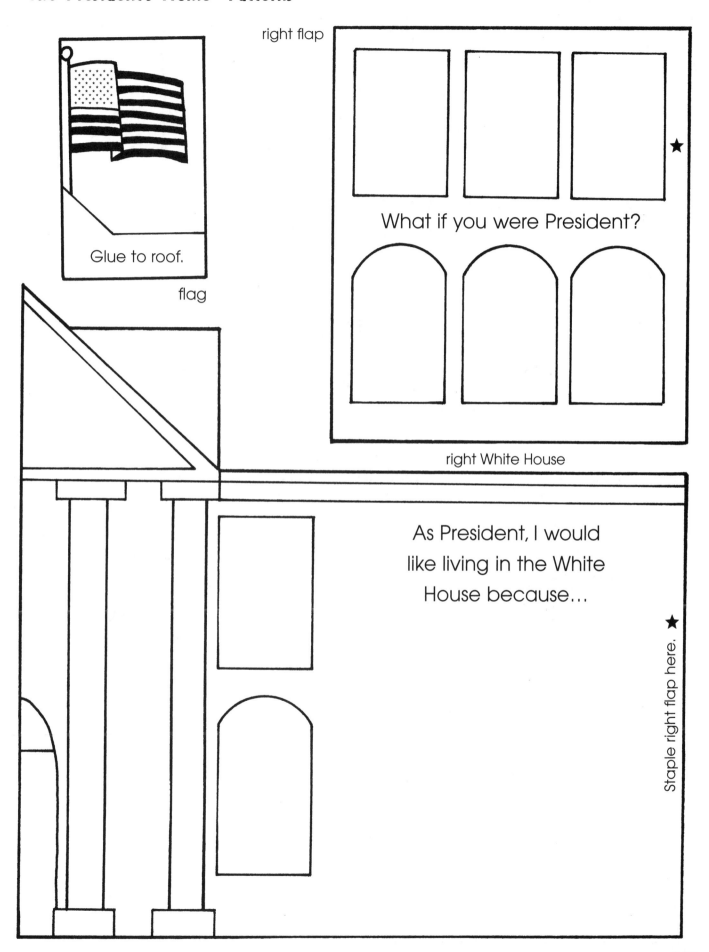

Glue to roof.

flag

right flap

What if you were President?

right White House

As President, I would like living in the White House because…

Staple right flap here. ★

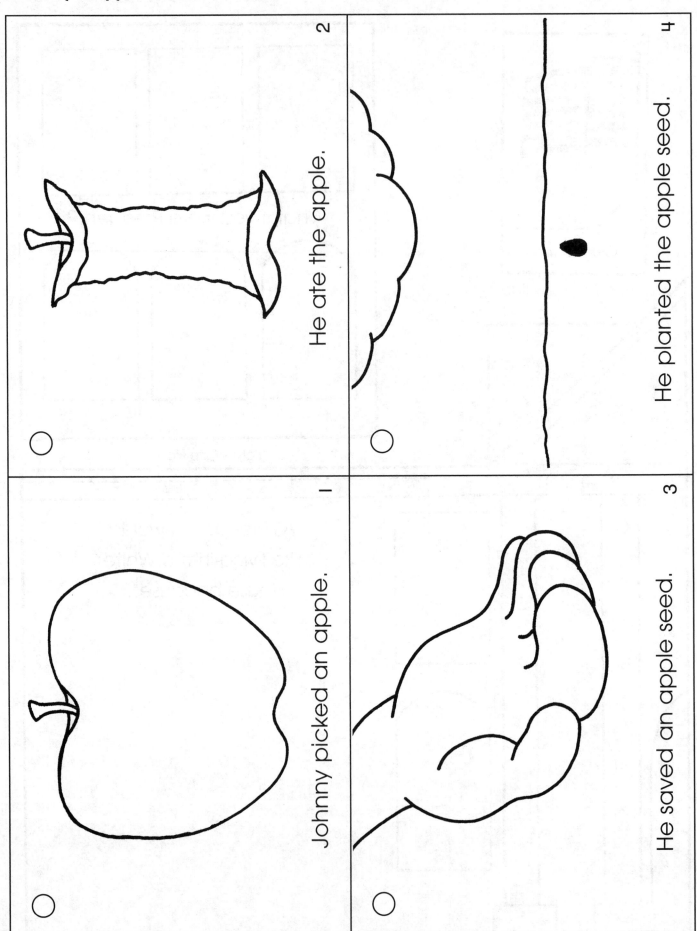

2

He ate the apple.

4

He planted the apple seed.

1

Johnny picked an apple.

3

He saved an apple seed.

"Johnny's Apple Seed" Patterns

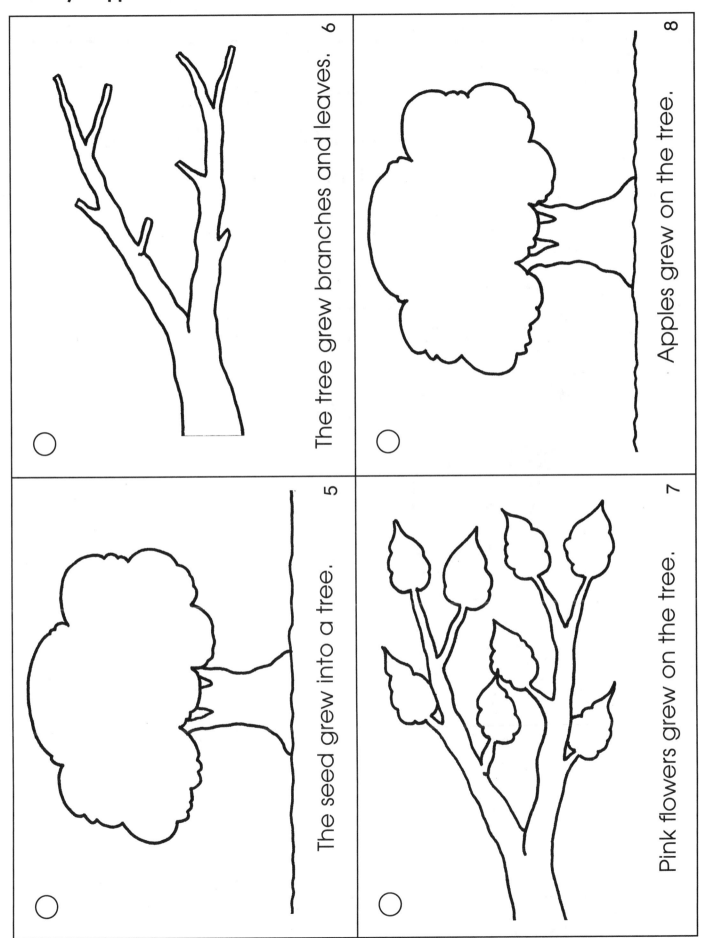

6

The tree grew branches and leaves.

8

Apples grew on the tree.

5

The seed grew into a tree.

7

Pink flowers grew on the tree.

Which president
put important papers
in his hat?

Abraham Lincoln!

5

Which president
is on the penny?

4

Which president
studied law on
his own?

3

Glue page 2 here.

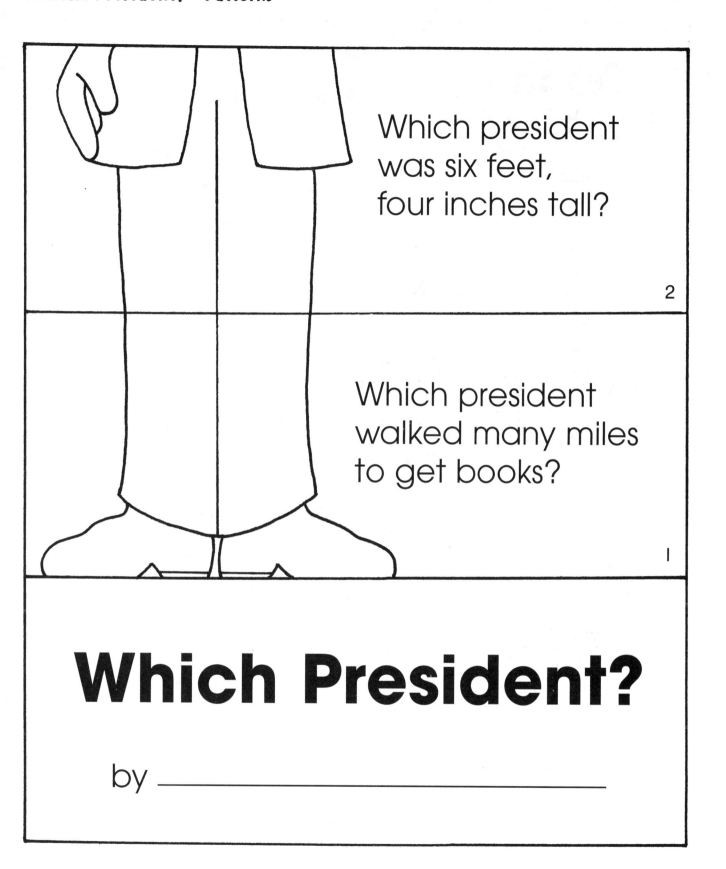

Which president
was six feet,
four inches tall?

2

Which president
walked many miles
to get books?

1

Which President?

by _____

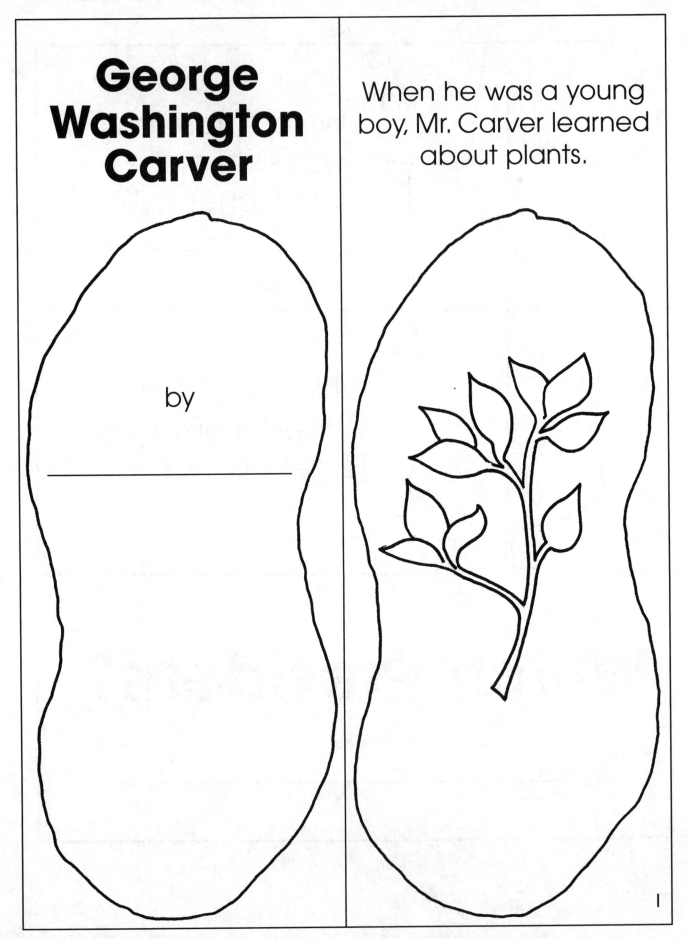

George Washington Carver

by

_____

When he was a young boy, Mr. Carver learned about plants.

1

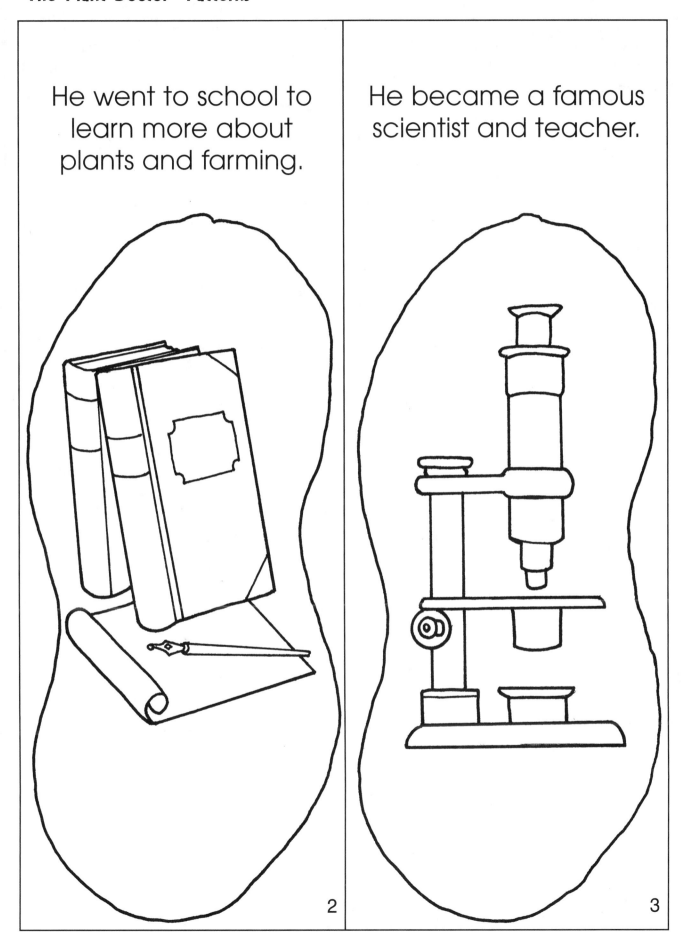

He went to school to learn more about plants and farming.

He became a famous scientist and teacher.

2

3

Staple pages here.

Mr. Carver invented many different things from peanuts.

4

"A Courageous Woman" Pattern

Rosa Parks was

_____

_____.

by _____

Staple pages here.

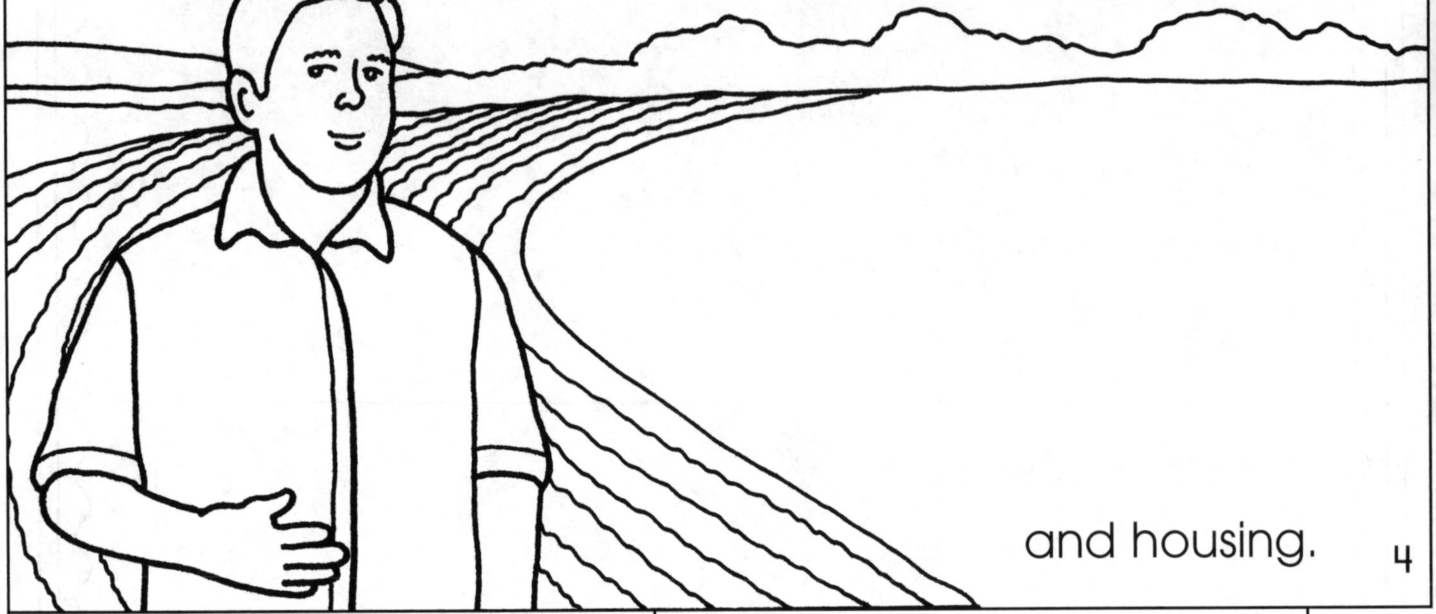

and housing.

4

1

Cesar Chavez helped farm workers get better . . .

3

pay.

Cesar Chavez

by _____

2

education,

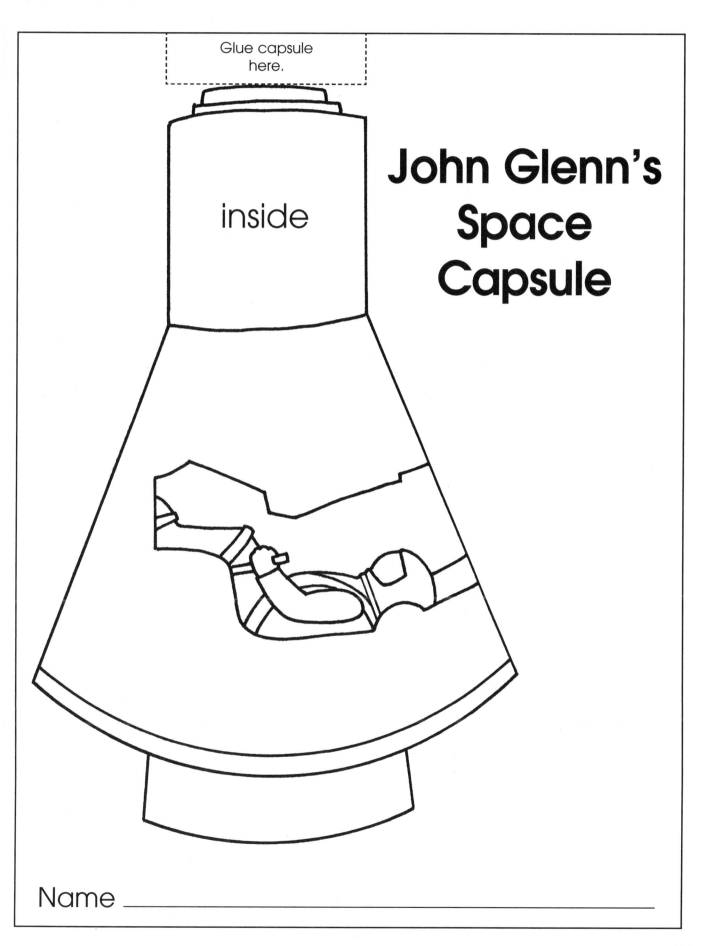

Glue capsule here.

inside

John Glenn's Space Capsule

Name _____

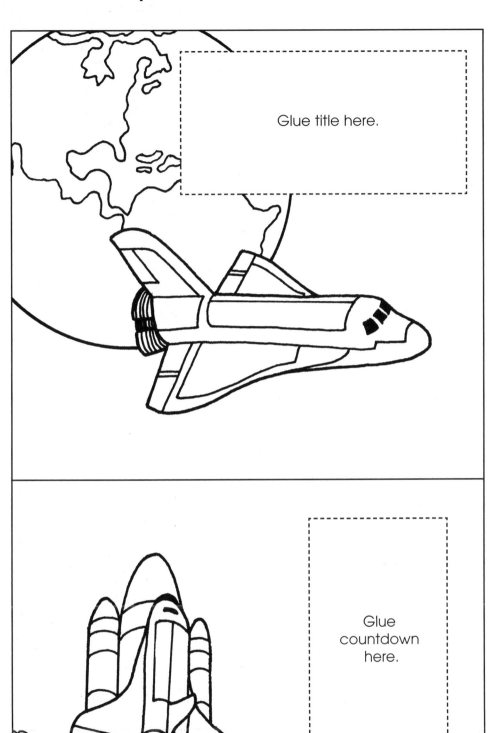

Glue title here.

Sally Ride's Space Trip

by _____

title

Glue
countdown
here.

BLAST OFF!

I

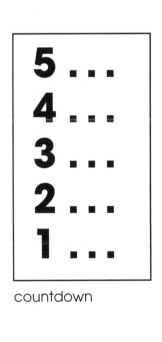

```
5 . . .
4 . . .
3 . . .
2 . . .
1 . . .
```

countdown

Glue space shuttle here.

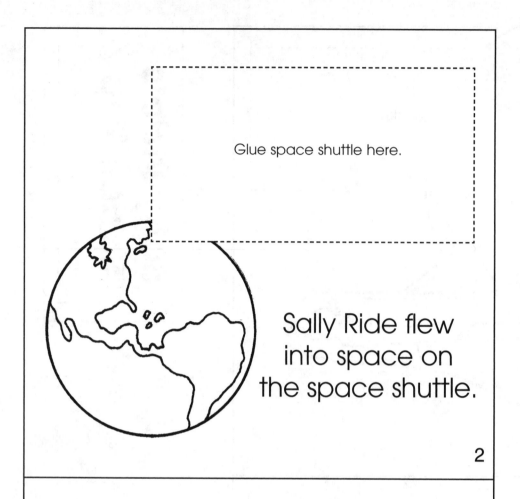

Sally Ride flew into space on the space shuttle.

2

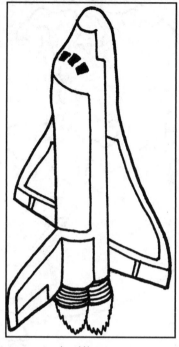

space shuttle

Glue window here.

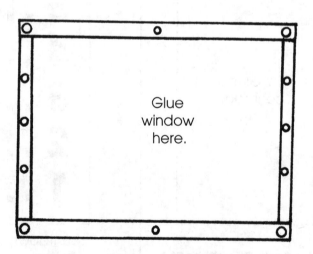

She ate, exercised, and slept in space.

3

window

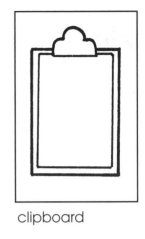

clipboard

She floated in space
to do her work!

4

Glue
Sally Ride
here.

Sally Ride

The first American
female astronaut.

5

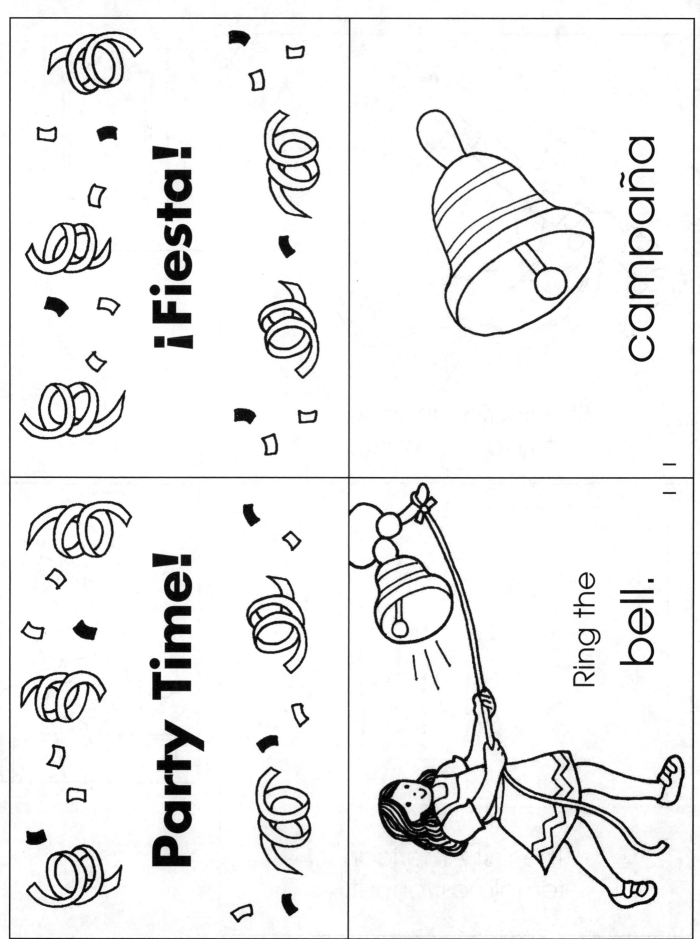

¡Fiesta!

campaña

_1_

Party Time!

Ring the
bell.

_1_

"Fiesta!" Patterns

bandera

2 2

música

3 3

Wave the
flag.

2

Listen
to the
music.

3

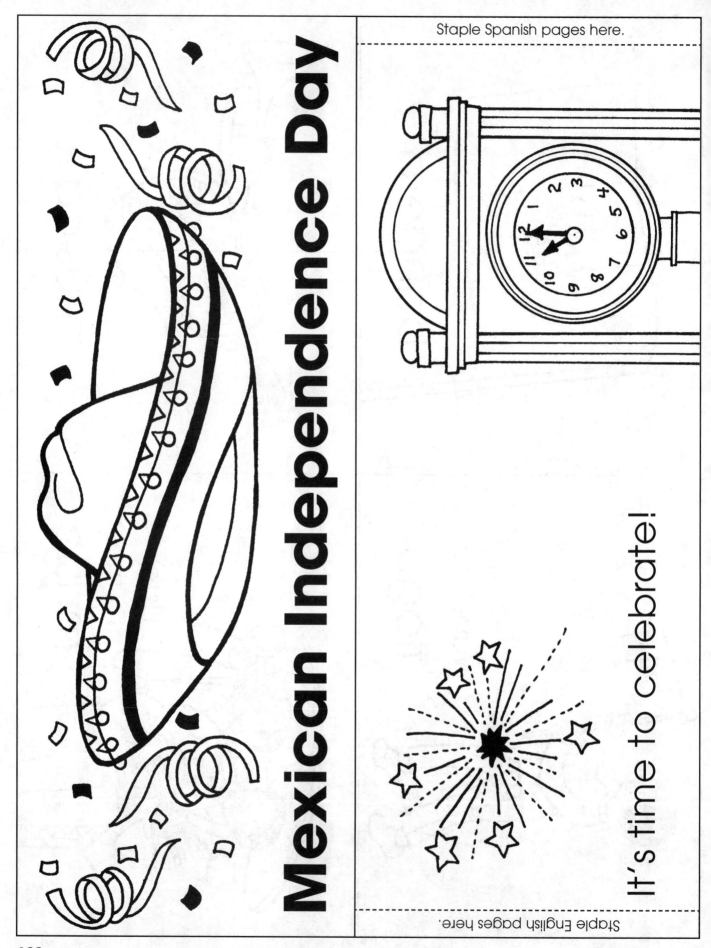

Mexican Independence Day

Staple Spanish pages here.

It's time to celebrate!

Staple English pages here.

Celebrate the Harvest!

by _____

Celebrate the rice harvest.

1

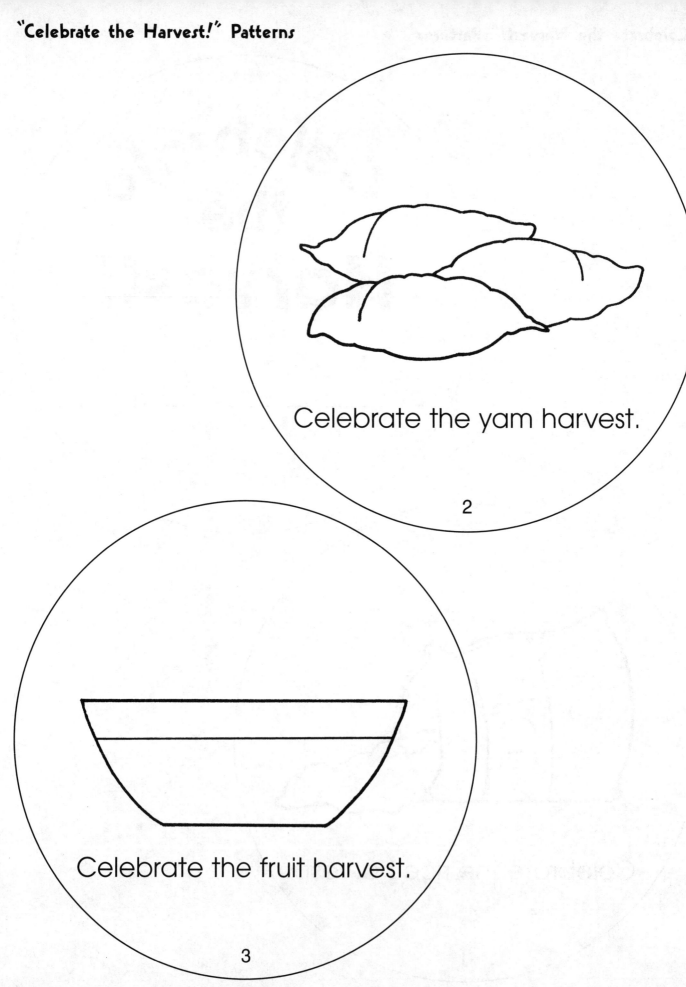

Celebrate the yam harvest.

2

Celebrate the fruit harvest.

3

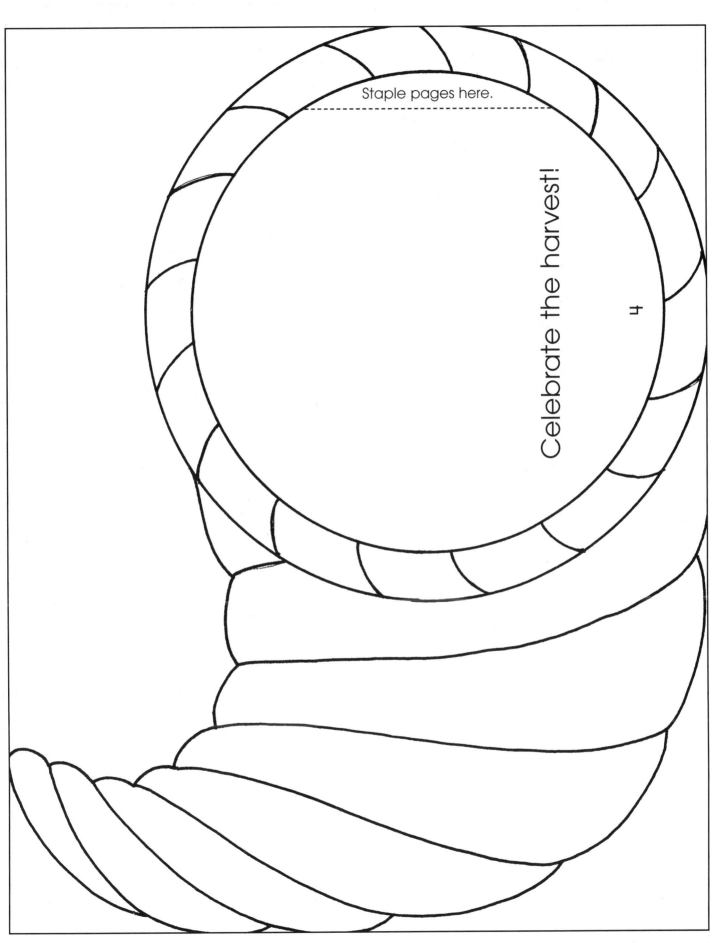

Staple pages here.

Celebrate the harvest!

4

Name _____

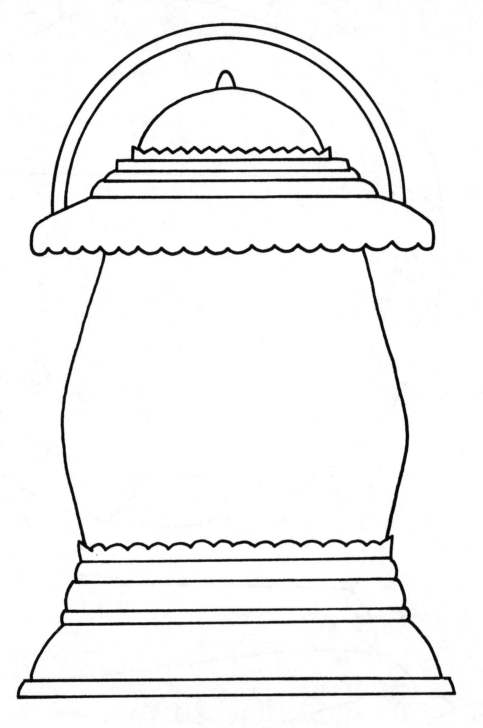

My lantern can

_____ in the night.

Diwali Lamp

by _____

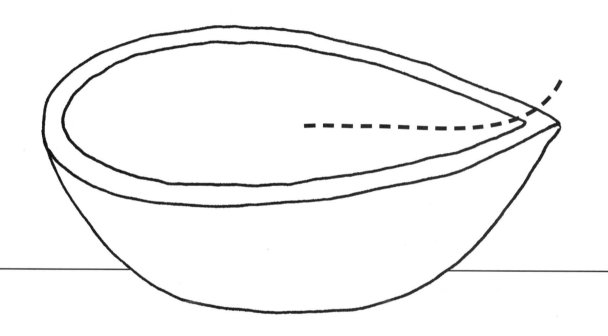

1. Color the lamp.

2. Add a wick.

3. Add oil.

4. Light the lamp.

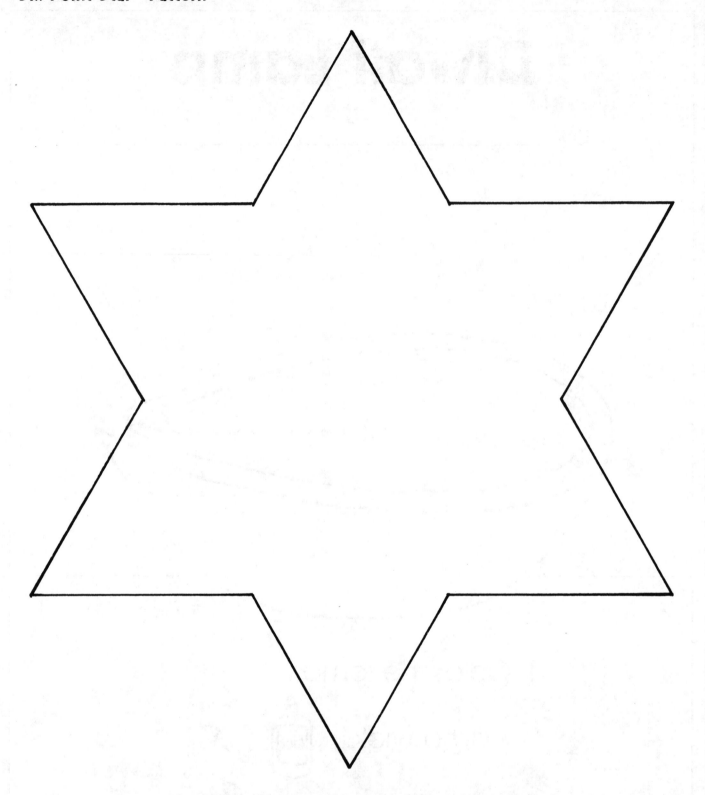

Six-point star sparkles so bright
on a special Hanukkah night.

"Christmas Lights" Patterns

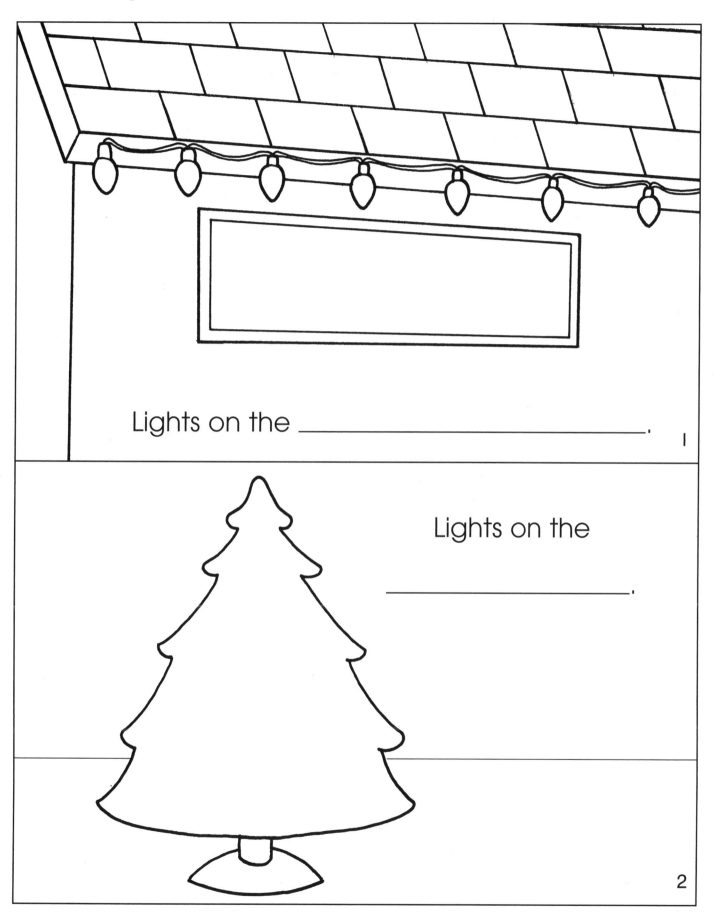

Lights on the _____. 1

Lights on the

_____. 2

Lights on the ————————.

3

A light
for

————————!

4

"Kinara Colors" Pattern

Name _____

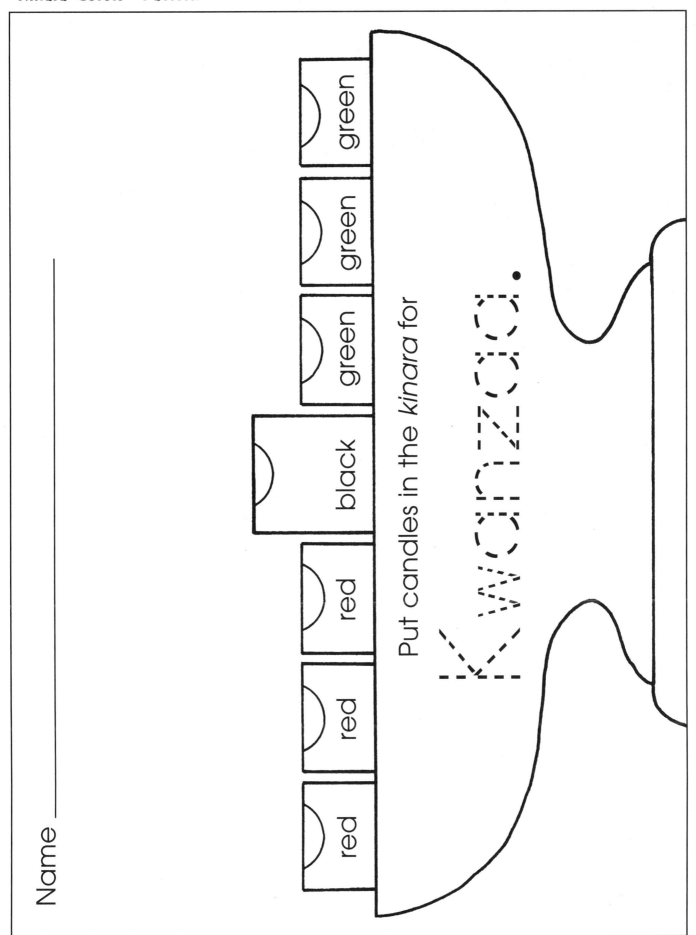

green green green black red red red

Put candles in the *kinara* for

Kwanzaa.

by _____

Happy New Year!

1

Horns honk.

Fireworks bang.

2

"New Year's Hat" Patterns

Staple here.

5

Happy New Year!

Old year: _____

New year: _____

Out with the old, in with the new.

4

3

Midnight is here.

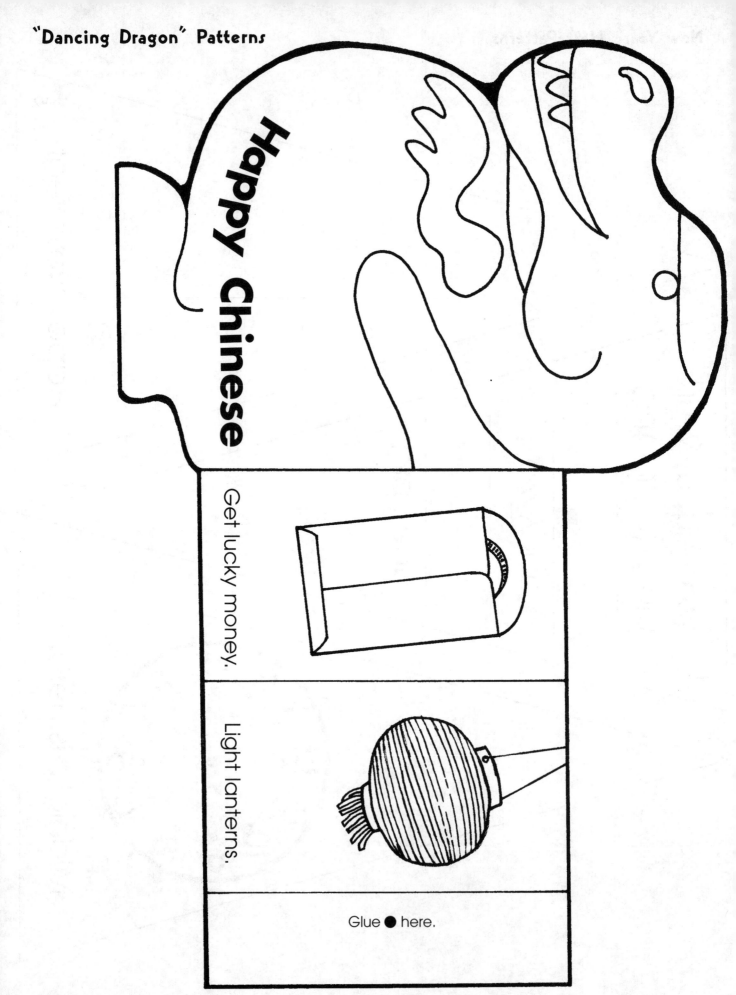

Happy Chinese

Get lucky money.

Light lanterns.

Glue ● here.

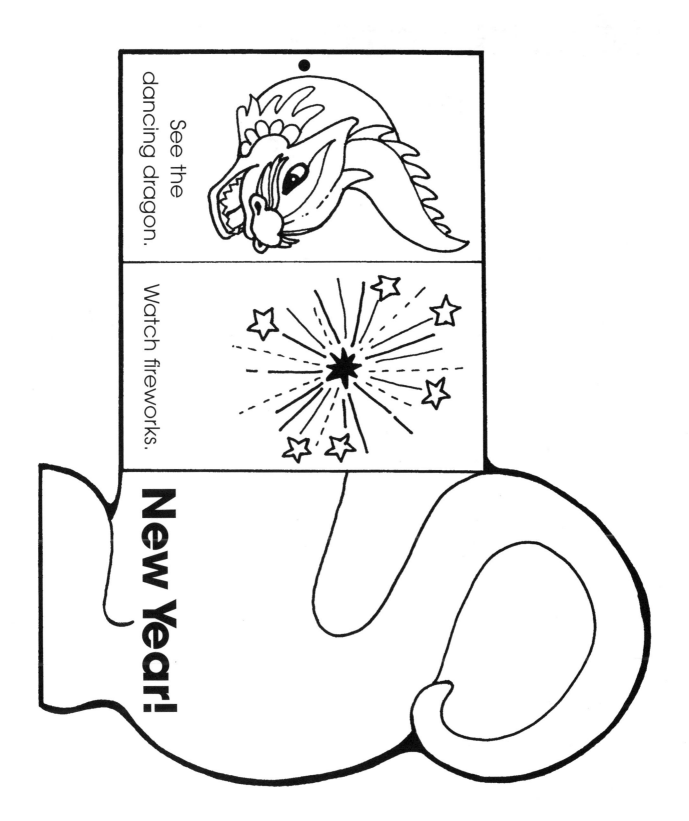

See the dancing dragon.

Watch fireworks.

New Year!

Masquerade Days

by _____

This is my
funny
Mardi Gras
costume.
I am a

_____.

This is my
scary
Karnavel
costume.
I am a

_____.

2

This is my
interesting
Purim
costume.
I am a

_____.

3

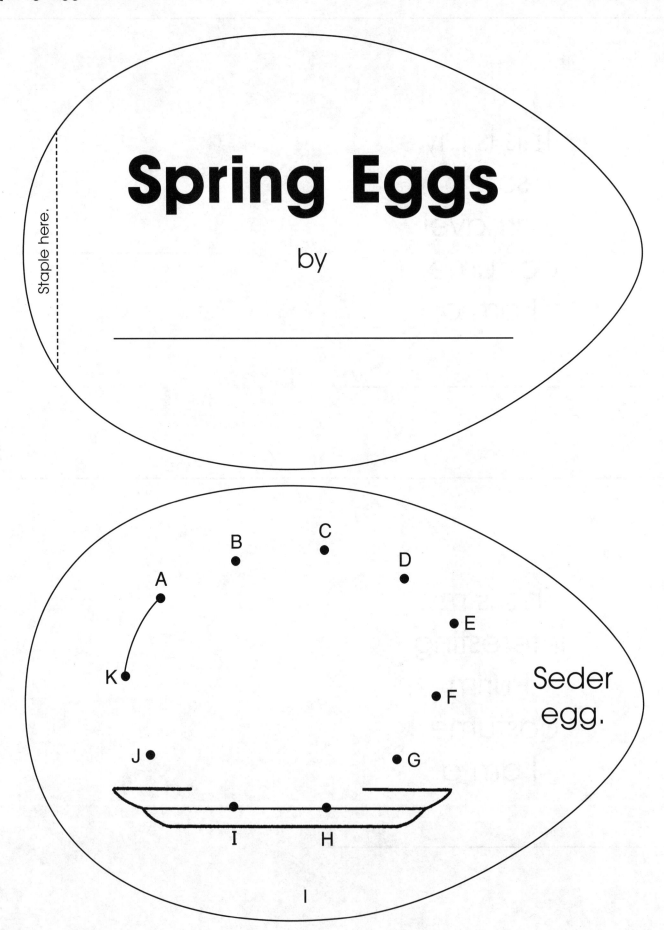

Spring Eggs

by

_____

Staple here.

A

B

C

D

E

K

F

Seder egg.

J

G

I

H

I

"Spring Eggs" Patterns

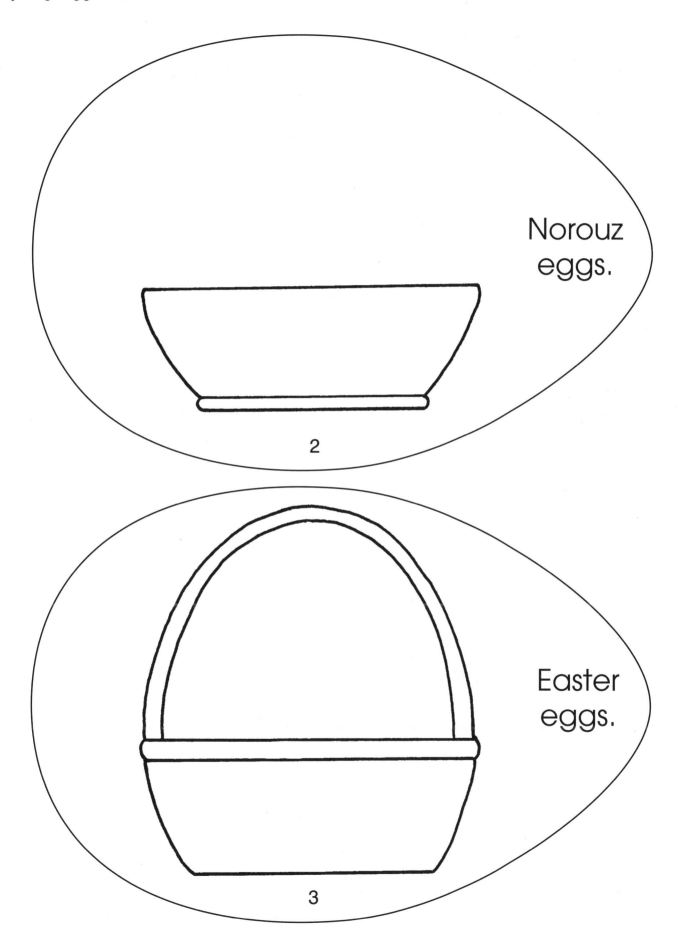

Norouz eggs.

2

Easter eggs.

3

"Spring Eggs" Patterns

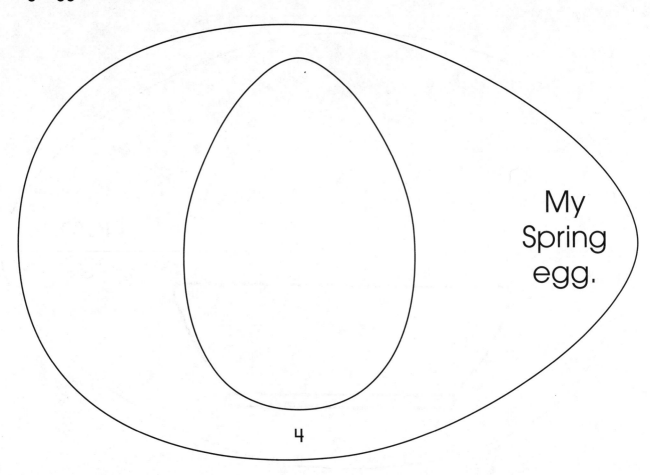

My
Spring
egg.

4

"Bilingual Piñata" Patterns

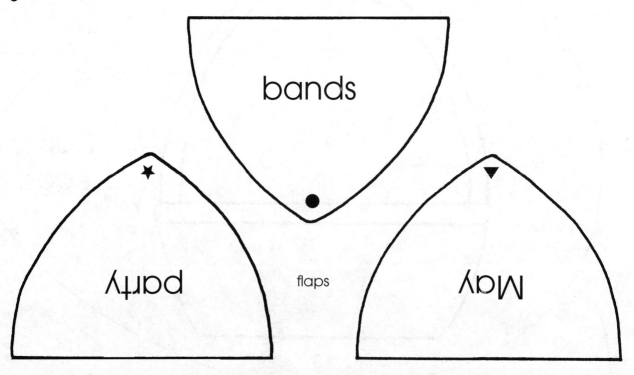

bands

party

flaps

May

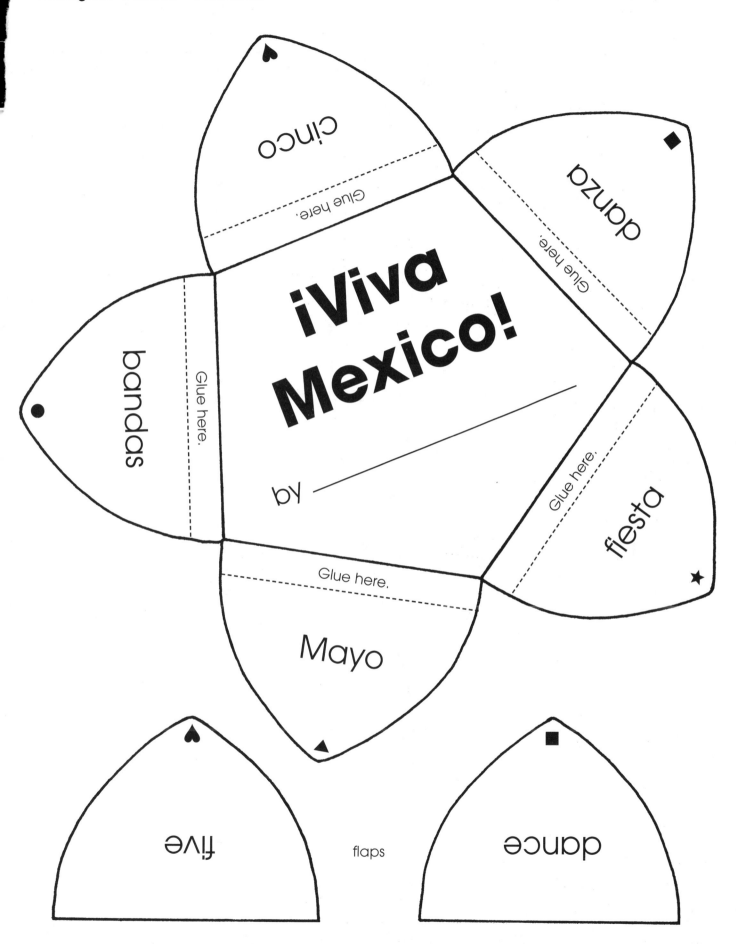

"Fish Flyer" Patterns

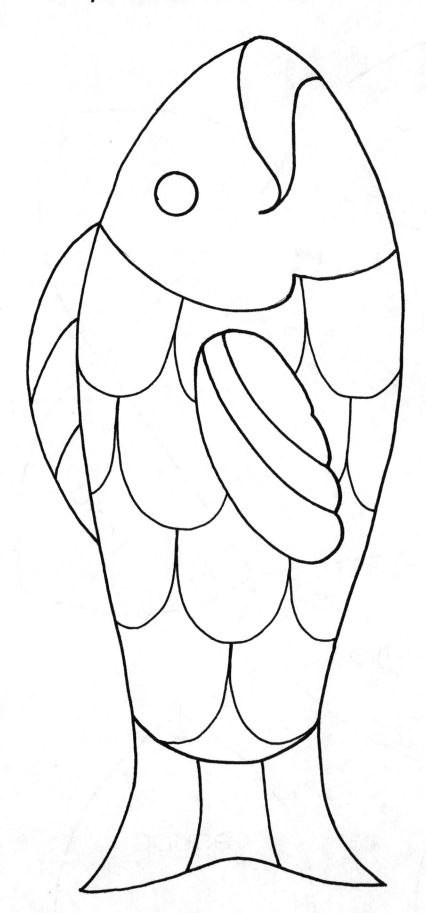

text box

I am as strong as a carp when I

by _____

"Fish Flyer" Patterns